Anita Lehmann • Jean-Baptiste Aubin • Joonas Sildre

# THE BIG BOOK OF PI

## The Famous Number You Can Never Know

HELVETIQ publishing has been supported by the Swiss Federal Office of Culture with a structural grant for the years 2026-2028.

With support from Forlen Stiftung and

ERNST GÖHNER
STIFTUNG

**The Big Book of Pi**
The Famous Number You Can Never Know

Author: © Anita Lehmann
Scientific writer: © Jean-Baptiste Aubin
Illustrations, cover design,
typesetting and layout: © Joonas Sildre
Editors: Aude Pidoux and Angela Wade
Proofreader: Theresa Cameron

ISBN: 978-3-03964-089-8
Third edition: 2026
Printed in China


Mittlere Strasse 4
4056 Basel
Switzerland

helvetiq.com

# MEET THE TEAM!

Anita
(who likes writing)

Jean-Baptiste
(who likes math)

Joonas
(who likes drawing)

Pi-Rat
(who likes asking questions)

Little Horsey PiPi
(who likes numbers)

When you see this icon, go to the Prove It chapter for further explanation.

# DEDICATIONS

**From Anita:**
To my mother Heidi, a natural mathematician.

**From Jean-Baptiste:**
To Esther, Leonora, Diane, and Leandro.

**From Joonas:**
To Joel, Ruuben, Taaniel, and Mirtel.

# THANKS

Thank you to the Swiss foundations who have supported us:
Loterie Suisse Romande, Ernst Göhner Stiftung, Forlen Stiftung.
Thank you to Sévérine Jacomy-Vité, Sibylle Ben Rhouma and Sandra Wirz from the Association La Chouette for their PI-votal support.
And thanks to Sam Williams for his close reading and for contributing materials to the educator's guide.

**From Anita:**
Thank you to my husband and children. My love for them is infinite.
Also many thanks to Wai Yi Feng for the mathematical first aid.

**From Jean-Baptiste:**
Thank you to Morgane and Yves for their careful proofreading, to my family for their unconditional support, and to my friends and colleagues for their encouragement.

**From Joonas:**
Thank you to my wife Elina.

# BIBLIOGRAPHY

A. S. Posamentier & I. Lehmann, *Pi: A Biography of the World's Most Mysterious Number*, Prometheus Books.
J.-P. Delahaye, *Le Fascinant nombre Pi*, Ed. Belin.

# TABLE OF CONTENTS

# CHAPTER 3.14

# INTRODUCTION

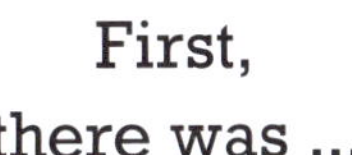

First,
there was ...

**A CIRCLE.**

A round thing.

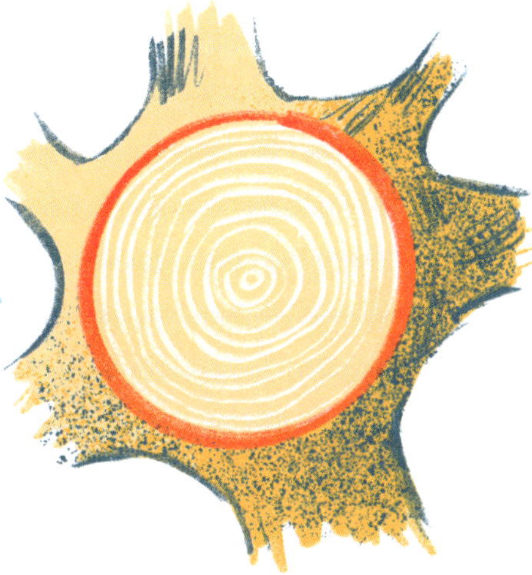

A wheel for a cart, maybe, or a hat. Or the moon at its fullest. The sun! A pan or a pot.

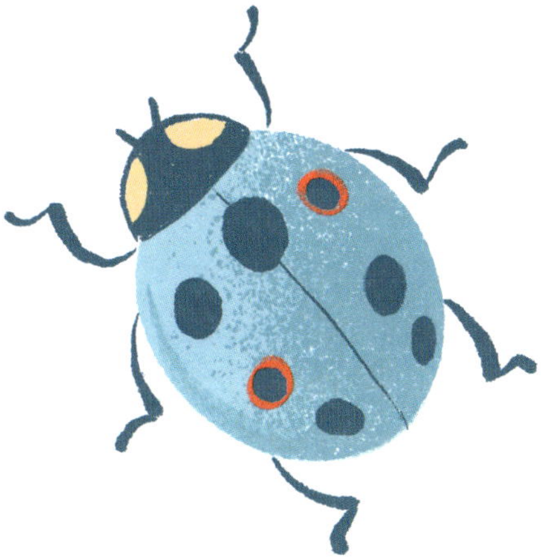

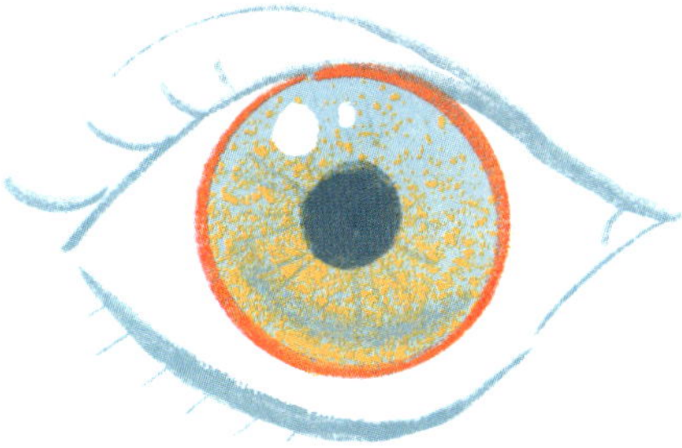

People worked with these round things, made them, measured them, and even tracked their movements in the sky. Soon, they noticed something INTERESTING.

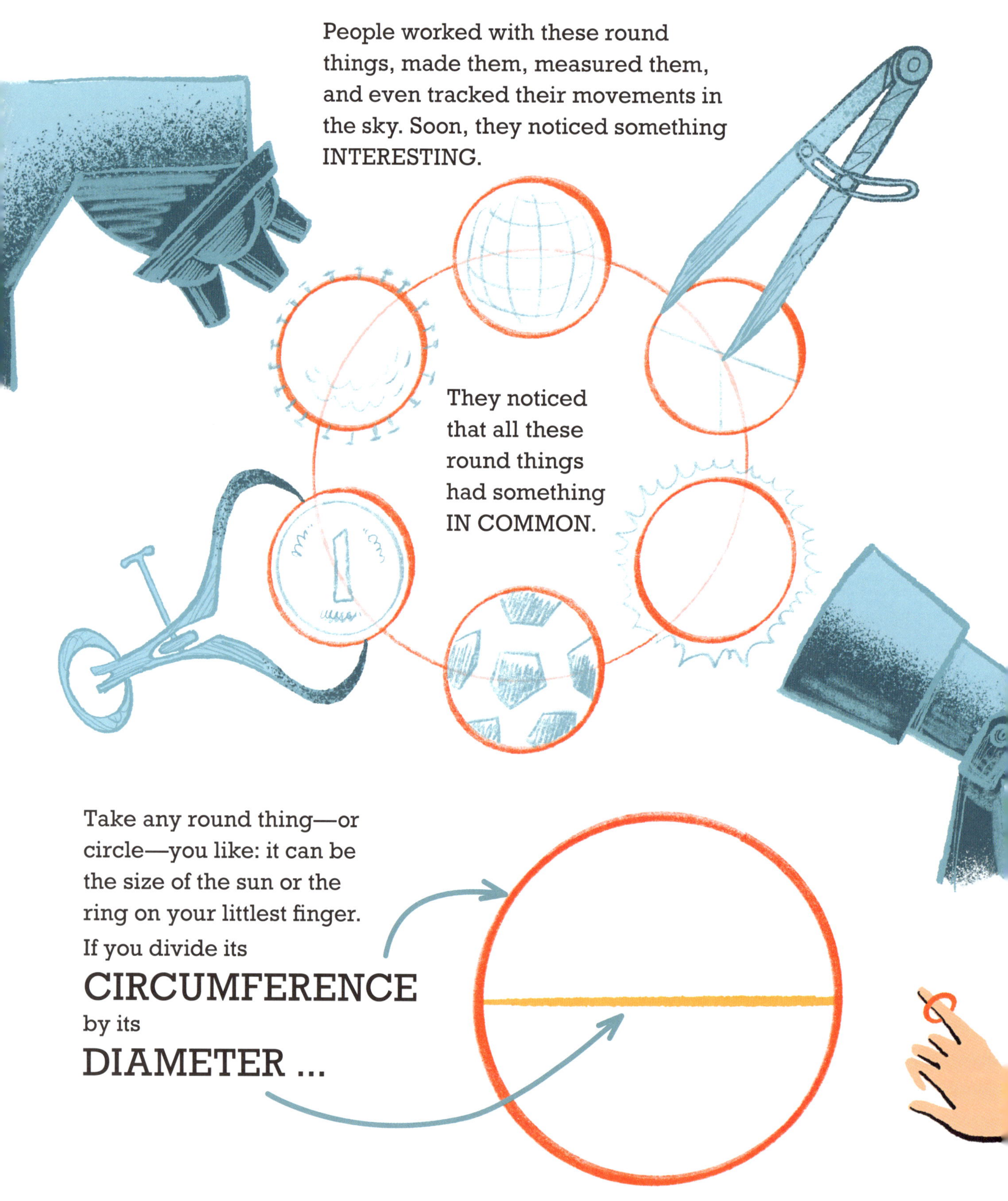

They noticed that all these round things had something IN COMMON.

Take any round thing—or circle—you like: it can be the size of the sun or the ring on your littlest finger.

If you divide its

CIRCUMFERENCE

by its

DIAMETER ...

**Circumference** is the distance around the outside of a circle.

**The diameter** is a direct line between two opposite points of a circle.

... you will find a mysterious number that is

# SOMEWHERE BETWEEN 3 AND 4.

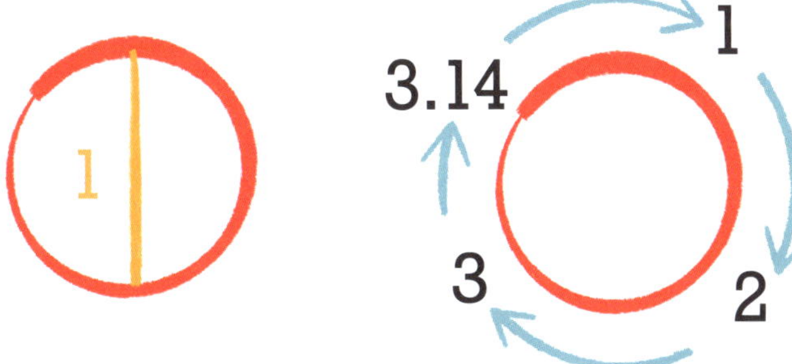


And this mysterious, constant number is called

**Pi.**

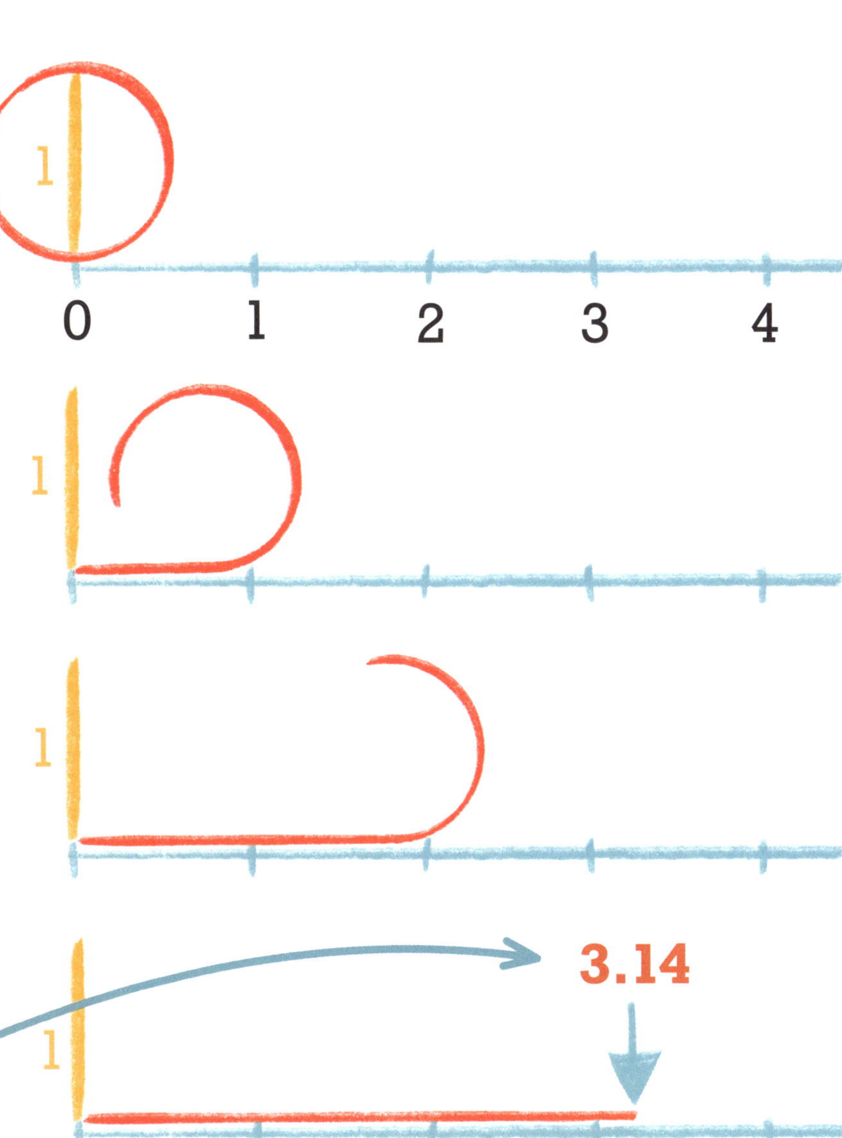


No matter how big or small the circle, the relationship between the circumference and the diameter is ALWAYS THE SAME.

It's a

## CONSTANT!

(a value or number that doesn't change)

**Pi** is the relationship between the circumference and the diameter of any given circle.

Here is the formula used to calculate the circumference:
**circumference = diameter x Pi**

WHY IS IT CALLED PI?
I'M SO GLAD YOU ASKED!
Well, in the old medieval days, mathematicians wrote to each other about circles all the time.
And instead of **Pi**, they wrote: *"Quantitas in quam cum multiflicetur diameter, proveniet circumferencia."*
This is medieval Latin. Translated it means:
*The quantity which, when the diameter is multiplied by it, yields the circumference.*
Oufff!! That's complicated!
Can you even imagine being a mathematician and EVERY TIME you want to share anything about circles you have to say
THAT SENTENCE?
No wonder people thought mathematicians were a bit ...
WEIRD!

# THEN ALONG CAME WILLIAM JONES ...

(1675-1749, from Wales)

He did a lot of exciting math with circles. He wanted to share his great thoughts with his friends.

So, he kept using THAT sentence:

Oh, you know: *The quantity which, when the diameter is multiplied by it, yields the circumference.*

There MUST be a way to talk about this constant without boring the pants off everyone!

So, one day (maybe in the bath, or sitting under a tree, or while eating his granny's delicious apple pie), he had an

**IDEA!**

Instead of saying:

Oh, you know: *The quantity which, when the diameter is* ... *the cir-*

I could make it MUCH SIMPLER.

I could just say:

**Pi!**

**Pi** is NICE AND SHORT.

# BUT WHY PI? WHY NOT CAKE ... or PUDDING?

**The perimeter** is the distance around the outside of a shape.

A circle's perimeter is exactly the same as its circumference!

Using Pi was a GREAT IDEA. Soon, everyone was using it, and people were really grateful to William, because now they didn't have to walk around saying:

The quantity which, when the diameter is multiplied by it, yields the circumference.

They could just say "Pi," and everyone knew what they meant, and this was extremely HELPFUL.

Pi

The authors of this book are grateful to William Jones for making their lives much SIMPLER. Thanks to him, the title of this book is not:

The Big Book of THE QUANTITY WHICH, WHEN THE DIAMETER IS MULTIPLIED BY IT, YIELDS THE CIRCUMFERENCE

Instead it is simply:

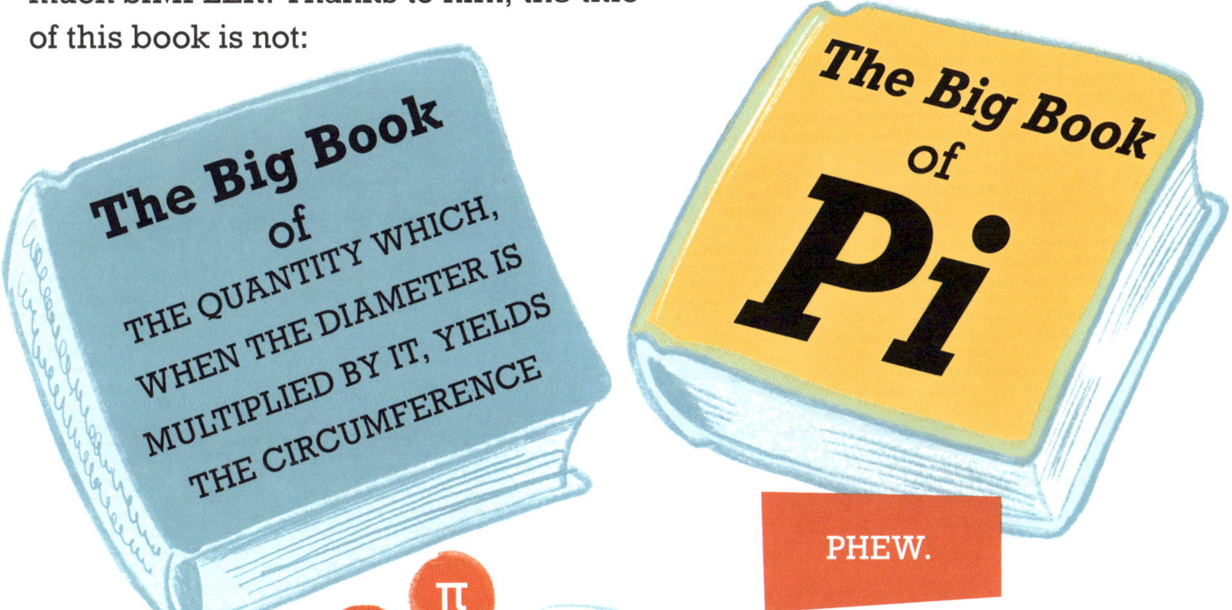

PHEW.

π π π π

The famous Swiss mathematician **Leonhard Euler** (1707–1783) was one of the first to adopt π in his work. Read more about him on p. 40.

# WHAT'S SO MAGICAL ABOUT PI?

OK. So Pi has something to do with circles and is a number somewhere between 3 and 4.

So what?

Well, even if you can't stand math, and even if you think Pi is stupid, the truth is:

YOU. CAN'T. ESCAPE. PI.

(Like, ever. Not even in the word stuPid. Ha! Did you notice?)
Even if you never have to deal with any circles, Pi turns up in lots of different, unexpected places—but more about that later.

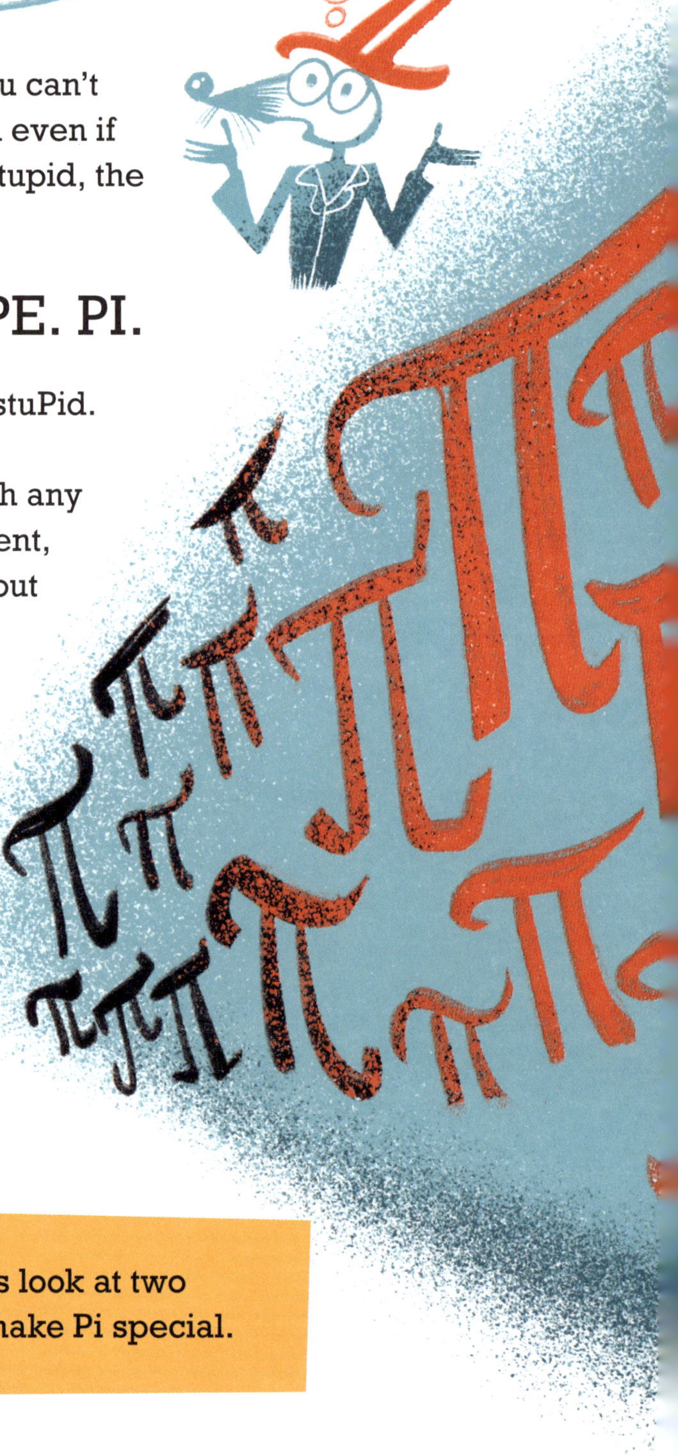

For now, let's look at two things that make Pi special.

# Pi is INFINITE*

Pi starts like this:

3.14

and then goes like this:

3.1415926

and then goes on like this:

3.141592653589

And then Pi just can't stop itself.

It goes on and on and on and on and on and on and on and on and on and on and on and on and on and on and on and on and on and on and on and on and on and on and on and on and on and on and on and on and on and on and on and on and on and on and on and on and on and on and on and on and on and on and on and on and on and on and on and on and on and on and on and on and on and on and on and on and on and on and on and on and on and on and on and on and on and on and on and on and on and on and on and on and on and on and on and on and on and on and on and on and on and on and on and on and on and on and on and on and on and on and on and on and on and on and on and on

Why should you never start talking to Pi at a party? Because it just goes on forever.

(Just like your boring uncle on Christmas Day...)

*Of course Pi isn't an infinite number, but its digits go on indefinitely. This is what we mean when we say "Pi is infinite" in this book.

**Fun fact: Pi in the stars!**

A few years ago, mathematician **Robert Matthews** (born 1959 in Britain) used probability to calculate an estimate of Pi by looking at how the stars are distributed in the sky ... and it worked! So, even the stars know about Pi!

PI is not only INFINITE.

## It's also IRRATIONAL

and therefore seriously COOL.

So, Pi is an IRRATIONAL number.
But what does that even MEAN?

I'M SO GLAD YOU ASKED!

It means that the decimals of Pi are not periodic.

Take a look at this number:

0.3333333333333333

You can see a certain pattern, right?
3 repeats, infinitely.

Mathematicians call this a **rational number**: a number sequence that repeats over and over again, infinitely.

Can you spot the pattern?

0.58 58 58 58 58 58 58

58 repeats and repeats ...

Or this one:

0.123 123 123 123 123 123

One, two, three, one, two, three, one two, three—like an infinite waltz.

How NICE of these numbers! So clear! So very RATIONAL!

**Decimals** help us write down a number that is not whole (i.e., not 1 or 2, but something in between). Take 1.3 for example. 1.3 is a number between 1 and 2. 3 is its first decimal.

**A waltz** is a sophisticated ballroom dance, where you move your feet to an endlessly repeating 1, 2, 3 rhythm and try not to step on your partner's toes.

Pi, by contrast, isn't NEAT like that. Pi is really TERRIBLE at having any kind of periodic pattern. Pi probably doesn't even know what a periodic pattern is (and, what's worse, doesn't CARE).

That's what makes Pi an IRRATIONAL number: it is infinite and non-repeating.

I mean, just look at the STATE of it:

3.1415926535
8979323846
2643383279
5028841971
6939937510
5820974944
59230781640628620899
8628034825
3421170679
82148
0865132
823066470938446095
5058223172
5359408128
481117450284102701938521105559
6446229489
5493038196442881
0975
6659
3344612847564
823378678
3165

... and then on it goes in its irrational ways ...

SO ANNOYINGLY IRRATIONAL!

**Irrational numbers** are all infinite, but not all infinite numbers are irrational. Fancy that!

Irrational numbers might be a bit WILD in that way and not super PRETTY to look at. But being irrational, Pi has COOLER things to offer than beauty!

Because Pi is irrational, you can find any number sequence you want in Pi. ANY!* That's pretty COOL. Let's take a look.

## FIND YOUR BIRTHDAY IN PI!

Think of your date of birth. Say it's August 28, 2015. In a number sequence, you might write it like this (month, day, year): 8.28.15. Then, you remove the dots and you get this:
82815

3.14

Guess what? You can find EXACTLY that sequence in Pi. Your birthday was written in Pi long before you were born.

If your birthday is indeed on August 28, 2015, you will find it at decimal no. 8776 in Pi.

You can find anyone's birthday in Pi! Try your own, your best friend's, your boring uncle's, your pet iguana's, Srinivasa Ramanujan's, Isaac Newton's, Beyoncé's, Ada Lovelace's, Katherine Johnson's...

You can find them all in Pi!

## IT'S NOT JUST BIRTHDAYS

You can also find your phone number, your Mum's credit card number, your passport number ...

You can find any number sequence of any length in Pi. Not only that, you can find that sequence an INFINITE number of times!

**Eek!**

Pretty cool, right? But wait, there's MORE ...

* It's fair to say that most mathematicians certainly BELIEVE that this is true for Pi, BUT because we know so very little, nobody has actually PROVEN it yet. Maybe you will?

# YOUR LIFE IN PI

If you assign each letter of the alphabet to a number sequence, you can find letters, words and entire books in Pi!

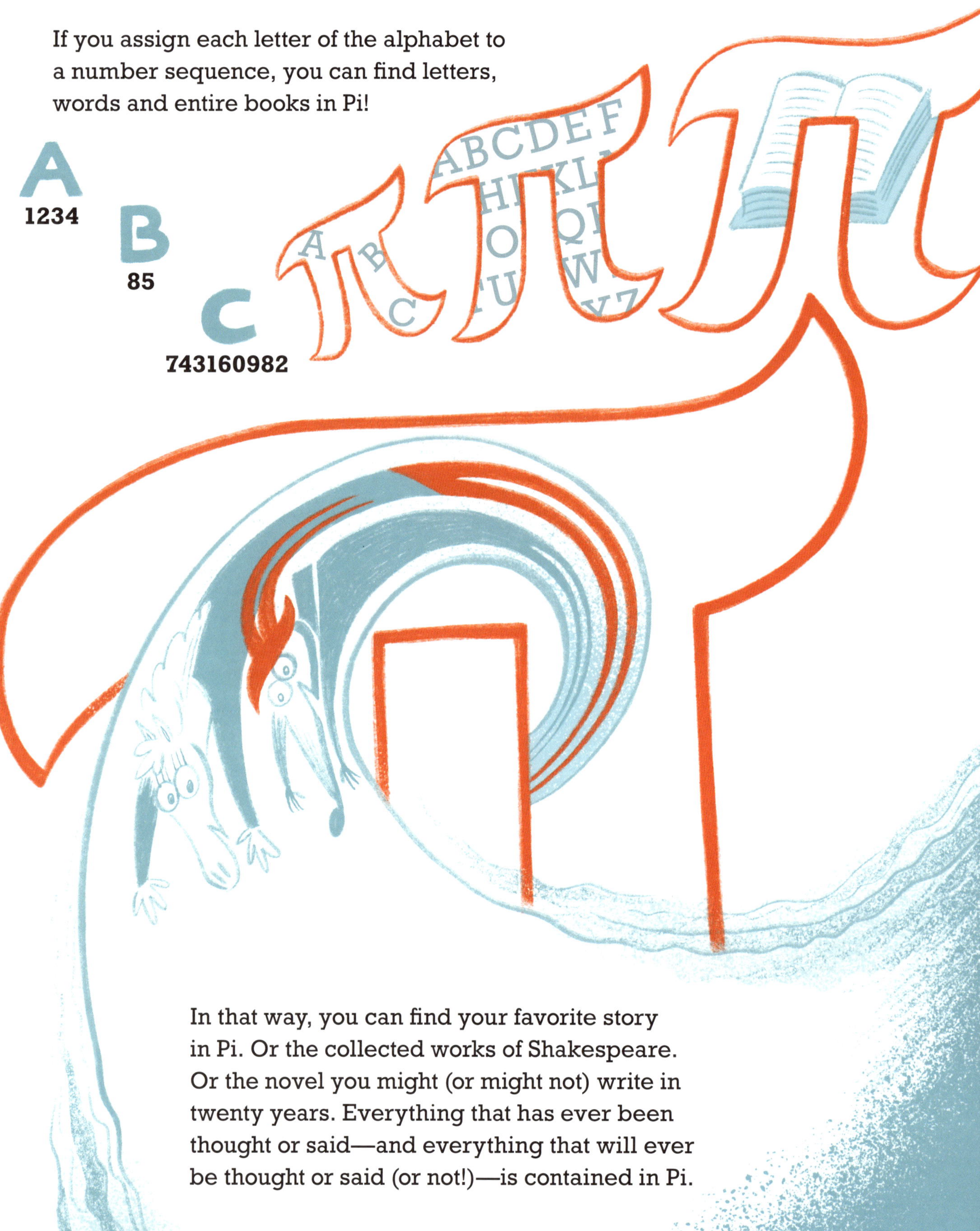


In that way, you can find your favorite story in Pi. Or the collected works of Shakespeare. Or the novel you might (or might not) write in twenty years. Everything that has ever been thought or said—and everything that will ever be thought or said (or not!)—is contained in Pi.

# AND THAT'S NOT ALL!

All the MUSIC and all the PAINTINGS and all the FILMS in the world can ALSO be found in Pi.

Simply assign a number to each musical note in a song, a number to each color (also called a pixel) that makes up a painting or each moment in a film …

**and BOOM.**

You will find exactly that number sequence in Pi—an infinite number of times.

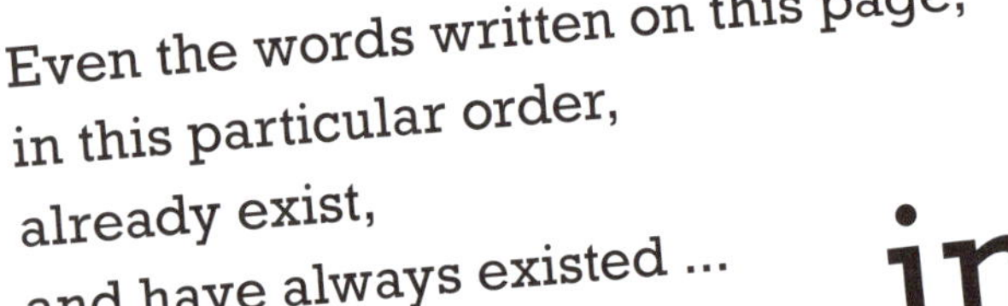


in

Pi!

The world is full of magical things patiently waiting for our wits to grow sharper.

**Bertrand Russell**
British mathematician
1872–1970

# CHAPTER 3.141

# PI STORY

Pi has been around since the dawn of time. It is hidden in every atom, every raindrop, and every dot on a ladybug's back. But for millions of years, the world existed quite happily without knowing about Pi. The dinosaurs certainly didn't care!

(OR MAYBE THEY DID??? What do you think?)

Then, along came HUMANITY.
With humanity came the first MATH NERDS.
And with the first math nerds came the first
**QUESTIONS**
about the mysterious constant Pi.

How much did we know about Pi around 4000 years ago? Turn the page to find out!

What humanity
knew about Pi
4000 years ago.

# THE FIRST MATH NERDS DISCOVER PI

We will never know who first stumbled over Pi. But we can make a pretty good guess as to HOW they stumbled over it.

A little HINT: it has to do with **CIRCLES!**

People have made calculations with circles for a very long time.

How else would you solve important problems such as how much copper you need to make a ring, how many stones for a sheep enclosure, or, most importantly, how much leather to make a **FOOTBALL?**

# THE ANCIENT BABYLONIANS

About 4000 years ago, the ancient Babylonians estimated Pi to be about 3.125.

Maybe they used this knowledge to build amazing things such as the Ishtar Gate's arch.

# THE ANCIENT EGYPTIANS

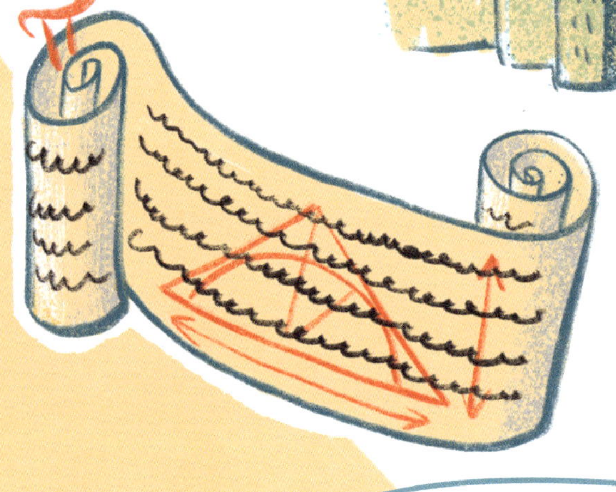

The ancient Egyptians also knew about Pi! We know this thanks to the Rhind Papyrus, which dates back to 1540 BCE.

It is OVER 16 FEET long and is full of formulas, information about the volume of pyramids, and also—you guessed it—the constant Pi!

Without the Rhind Papyrus, we would know even less about ancient Egyptian math.

The Egyptians probably used 256/81 as an estimate for Pi, which is around 3.16. Some historians think that this ratio was found because of the ancient game of mancala, which uses circles.

PROVE IT

This just goes to show that playing is an excellent way of learning new things!

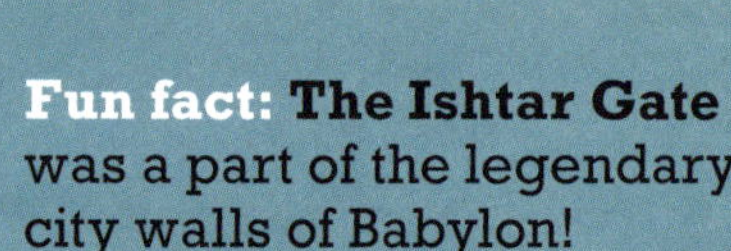

**Fun fact: The Ishtar Gate** was a part of the legendary city walls of Babylon!

It was clear now that Pi was an important, intriguing number that helped people build brilliant arches and draw excellent circles …

But the ancient math nerds also knew that their calculations were not very **PRECISE.**

And that **BOTHERED** them.

"A number somewhere around 3.1" might be a good enough answer for some, but **NOT FOR MATHEMATICIANS!**

Mathematicians like PRECISION, and Pi was not playing along!

It was all very frustrating.
And then, along came … Archimedes!

**Fun fact:** If you divide the perimeter of the base of the **Great Pyramid of Giza** by twice its height, you get a really accurate estimate of Pi.
$(4 \times 230)/(2 \times 147) \approx 3.13$

A happy accident of architecture? Or did the ancient Egyptians know more than we think?
What do you reckon?

# "DON'T MESS WITH MY CIRCLES"

**Archimedes** was a serious math geek who lived 2300 years ago, in Syracuse, Sicily.

Some people say that Archimedes was the greatest mathematician of his time. Others say he was the greatest mathematician

OF ALL TIME.

(Those people clearly haven't met YOU yet, have they?)

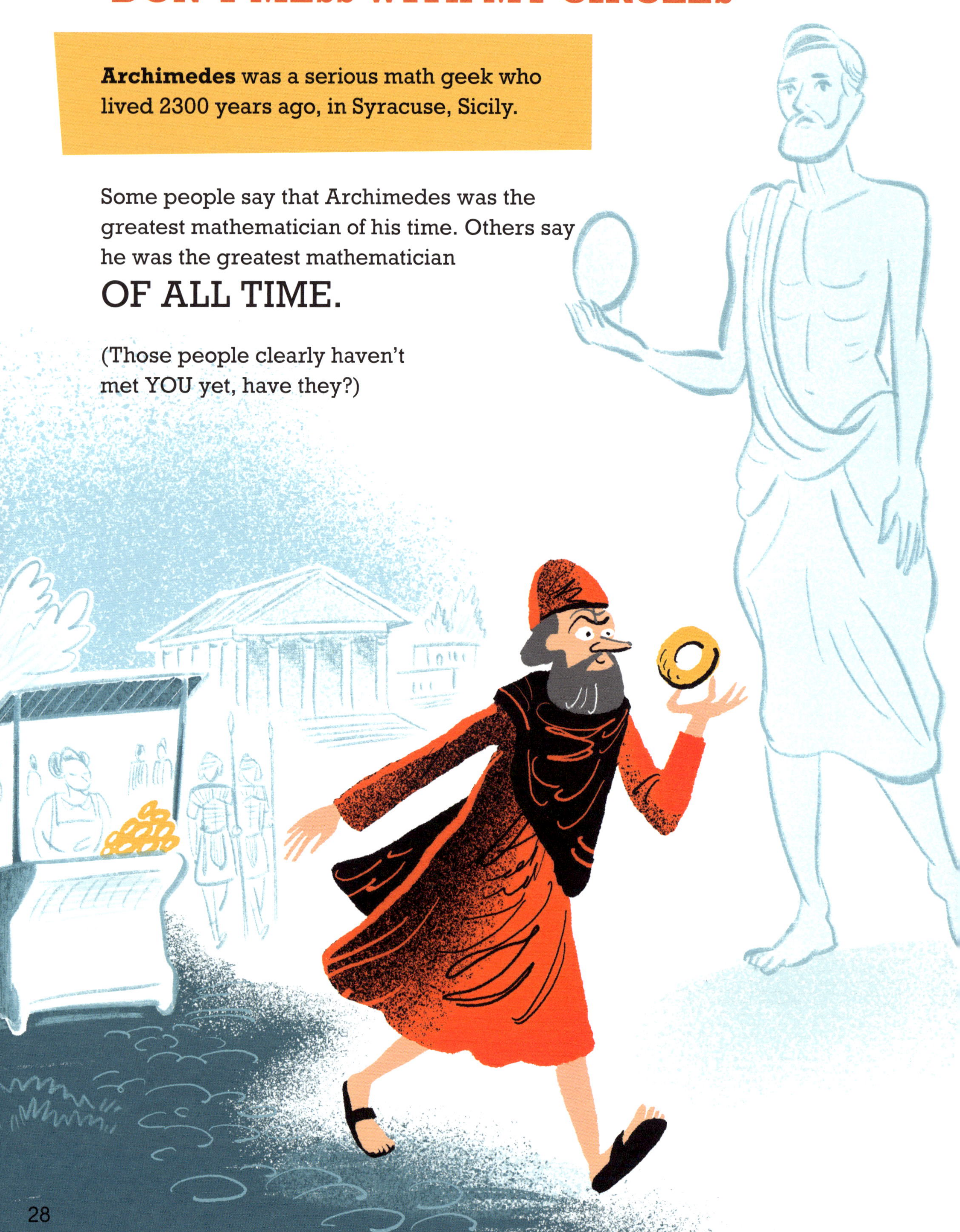

Archimedes loved everything to do with math, but circles were his passion. He was **OBSESSED** with circles.

Because he wanted to do calculations with circles, he needed to better understand Pi—and be more **PRECISE.**

So, he devised a **CLEVER PLAN.**

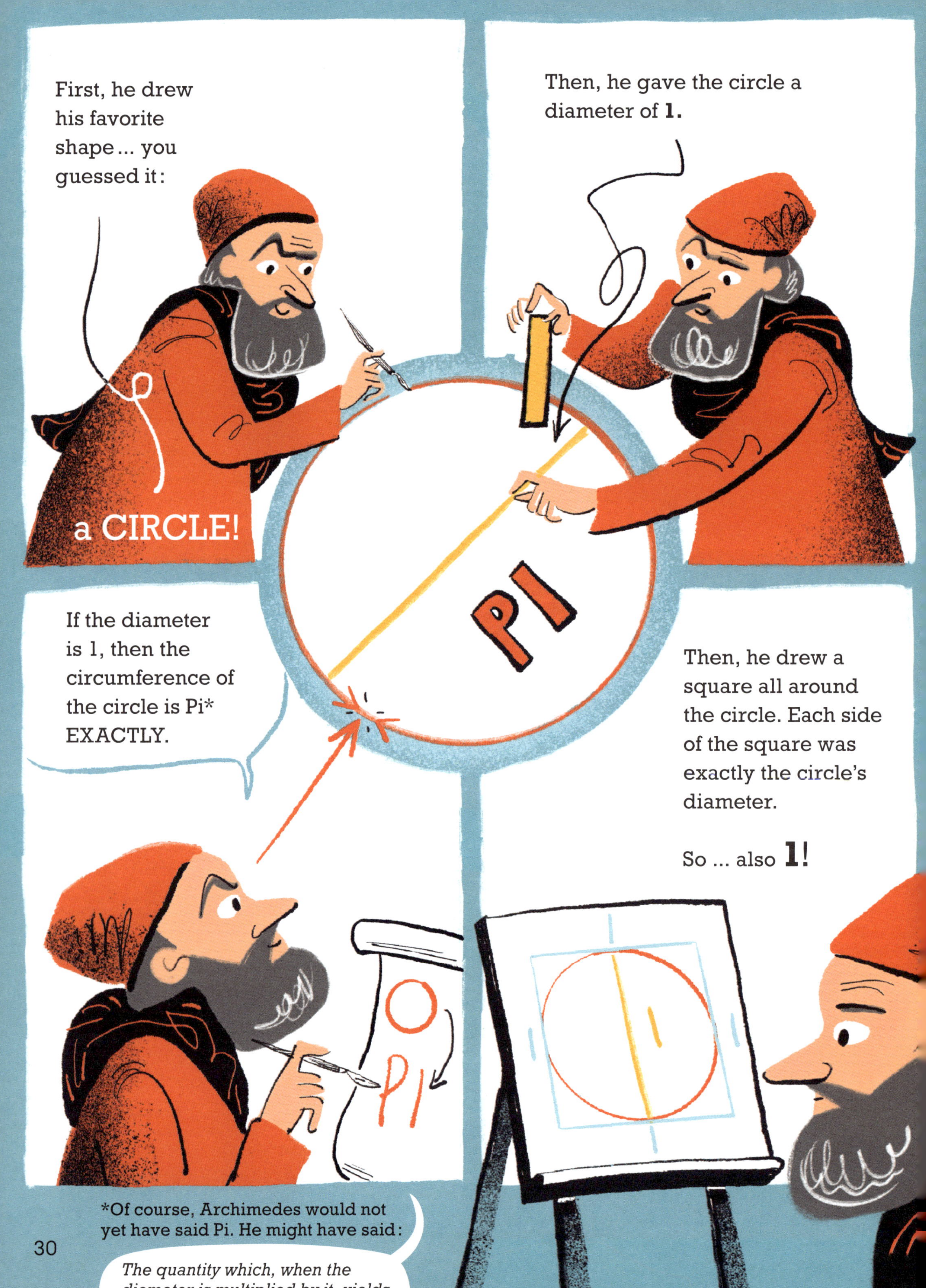

First, he drew his favorite shape... you guessed it:
a CIRCLE!
Then, he gave the circle a diameter of **1.**
PI
If the diameter is 1, then the circumference of the circle is Pi* EXACTLY.
Then, he drew a square all around the circle. Each side of the square was exactly the circle's diameter.
So ... also **1**!
PI
1
*Of course, Archimedes would not yet have said Pi. He might have said:
*The quantity which, when the*

Archimedes then added up the four sides of the square:

Just by looking at it, you can tell that the circle is "smaller" than the square.

Thus, the circumference of the circle is smaller than the perimeter of the square—smaller than 4!

Archimedes had his first exciting insight: Pi must be smaller than 4!

THEN, Archimedes drew another square, but this time, he put it INSIDE the circle. Then, he calculated the perimeter of THAT square, which turned out to be 2.828.

For obvious geometrical reasons, the square's perimeter is SMALLER than the circle's circumference, because it sits INSIDE the circle.

So, its perimeter is SMALLER THAN PI.

So Pi must be bigger than 2.828, but smaller than 4.

**GO, Archimedes!**

Archimedes kept going with his calculations. He added more sides to the square, and thus turned the square into a POLYGON with more than four sides.

He kept going, until he had drawn a 96-SIDED POLYGON inside the circle. This helped him get closer and closer to the value of Pi, but he couldn't work it out exactly.

Archimedes was probably a bit of a perfectionist, so that must have been FRUSTRATING for him.

Using his 96-sided polygon, he calculated that Pi must be

## BIGGER

than 3.14 and

## SMALLER

than 3.15.

Thus, Archimedes played a BIG ROLE in getting closer to finding Pi's hidden decimals...

**A polygon** is a shape with three or more straight sides—like a triangle or a square.

# THANK YOU, ARCHIMEDES!

Now, Archimedes might have been a fantastic mathematician, but he met a GRISLY END.

He had just drawn some gorgeous circles and was getting into some lovely calculations, when Roman soldiers burst into his home in 212 BCE and killed him.

That's how **IMPORTANT** circles were to him.

Would YOU die to protect some circles?

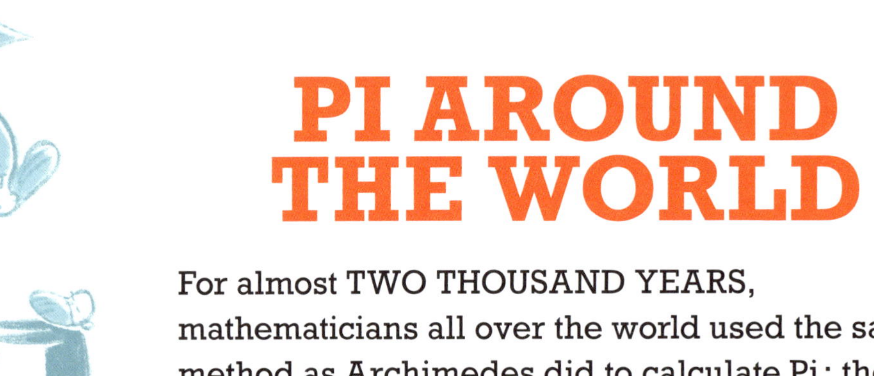

# PI AROUND THE WORLD

For almost TWO THOUSAND YEARS, mathematicians all over the world used the same method as Archimedes did to calculate Pi: they took a polygon and gave it more and more sides in order to get closer and closer to Pi. Because

EVERYONE

wanted to get to the bottom of Pi!!

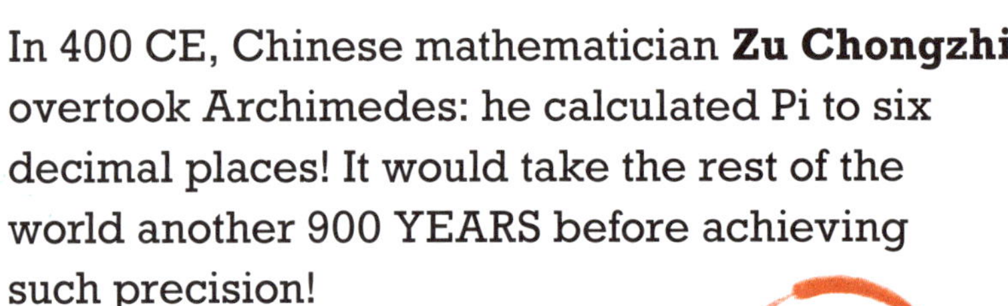

In 400 CE, Chinese mathematician **Zu Chongzhi** overtook Archimedes: he calculated Pi to six decimal places! It would take the rest of the world another 900 YEARS before achieving such precision!

In India, **Aryabhata** lived around 500 CE. He used the same method as Archimedes to find four decimal places (3.1416). With that, he estimated the circumference of Earth. He got it right to within 70 miles … all without a calculator!

**Jamshid al-Kashi** (1380–1429), an astronomer working in Samarkand, Uzbekistan, used a polygon with—wait for it—805 MILLION sides! Without a computer! This way, he found 14 decimal places of Pi.

3.14159265358979

And what was happening in the AMERICAS, you ask? You know the MAYANS, that amazing civilization whose astronomers predicted the movements of stars with incredible

# PRECISION?

Well, sadly we'll never know about the Mayans' understanding of Pi, because when the Spanish conquered the Mayan territory in the 16th century, they decided to burn all the Mayan books—which contained the knowledge of an entire people. Only a very few survived, and we lost almost an entire civilization's wealth of understanding about math, astronomy, culture and religion …

So we'll never know what the Mayans knew or thought about Pi. It's a crying shame.

After Archimedes, the EUROPEANS didn't really do much more with Pi for centuries. Partly, this had to do with THE BIBLE, the holy book for Christians, which mentions Pi.

## PI IN THE BIBLE!

In the olden days, people were sure that everything in the Bible was 100% true.

**BUT …**

In 1 Kings 7:23, you'll find the following words describing Pi:

"ten cubits from brim to brim, circular in form, with a circumference of thirty cubits."

… which is a roundabout way of saying that Pi is exactly 3. Right?
No! Wrong!

Pi = 3 is very wrong!

This made life very tricky for mathematicians! They could PROVE that Pi was not 3, but they couldn't say anything. Because if they did, they might get into

**BIG TROUBLE!**

Would you be willing to die for telling the truth about Pi?

Luckily, by the time German **Ludolph van Ceulen** (1540–1610) came along, it was OK to say that the Bible didn't always get things exactly right.

Ludolph loved fencing, math ... and Pi. When he wasn't fencing, he spent his entire time calculating Pi's decimals.

Guess how many sides Ludolph's polygon had?

**515 BILLION SIDES!**
Can you even IMAGINE?

With that, Ludolph calculated Pi up to 34 decimal places!

Ludolph loved Pi so much that after his death, Pi was engraved on his tombstone.

And his mathematical fame was such that in Germany, some people still call Pi "the Ludolphine number."

# DIGGING DEEPER: 15th to 18th CENTURIES

## MADHAVA OF SANGAMAGRAMA WORKS WITH INFINITY

In the late Middle Ages, the mathematician and astronomer **Madhava of Sangamagrama** (c.1350–1425) from Kerala, India, came up with a completely new way of calculating Pi.

Madhava's idea was to use
**INFINITY**
to get a formula for Pi.

Before Madhava, people used Archimedes' method—i.e., GEOMETRY—to calculate Pi. Madhava came up with a new tool. And that tool was called CALCULUS.

P! PROVE IT

**Calculus** is a branch of mathematics where you can make calculations with infinitely small quantities.

**Disclaimer:** Of course it's possible that someone other than Madhava first came up with calculus, but he's the first one **we know about.**

He worked out Pi's decimals by adding and subtracting fractions to get closer and closer to the true value of Pi—all the way to infinity!

Look at how pretty his formula looks:

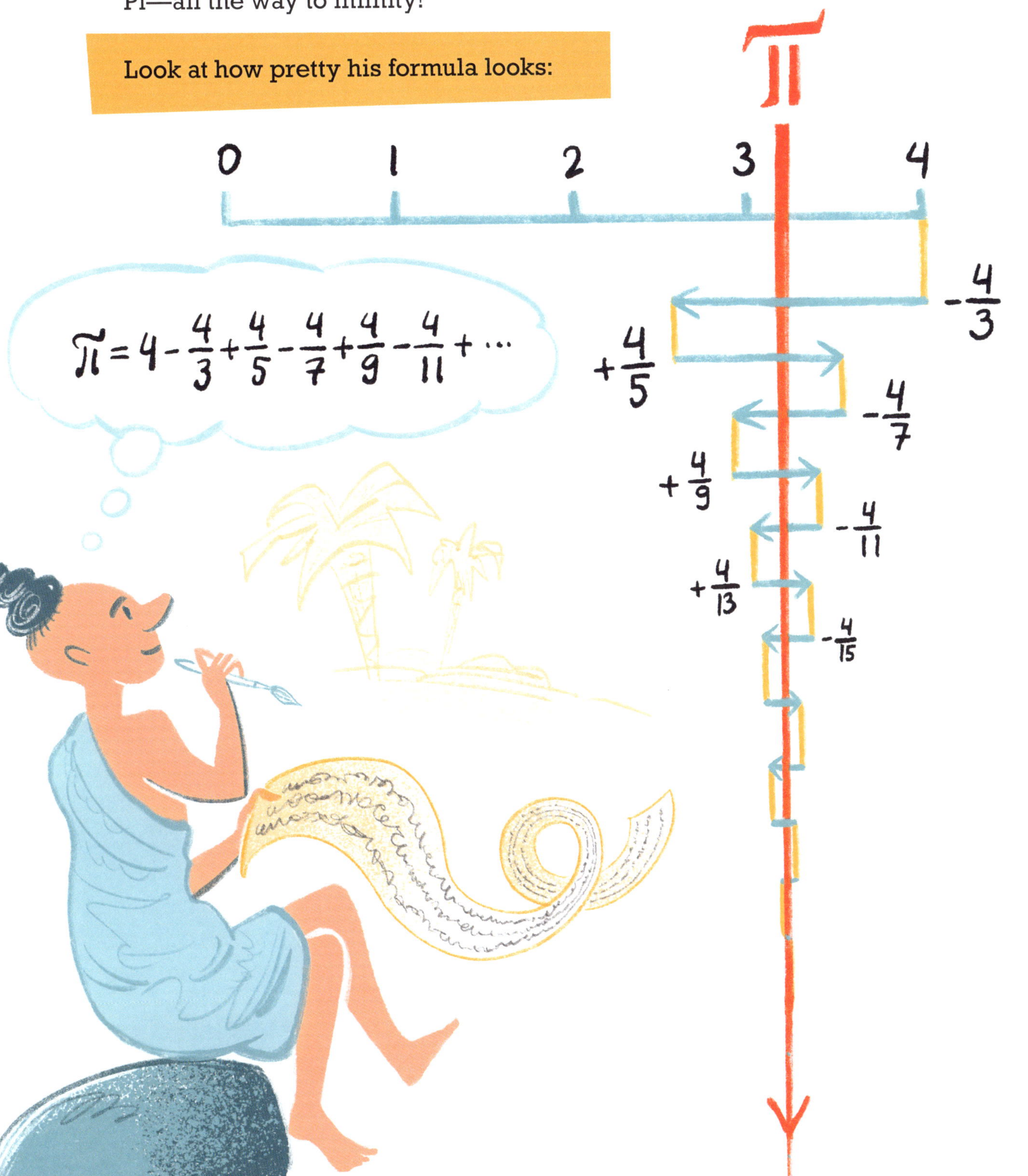


**Fun fact:** Madhava and his colleagues wrote on **palm leaves** instead of paper. And they didn't use NUMBERS. They wrote all the formulas down in VERSE, like a poem.

**Fun fact:** This is sometimes called **Madhava-Gregory-Leibniz's formula**, because 200 years after Madhava, European scientists Gregory and Leibniz came up with exactly the same formula!

# EUROPE CATCHES UP: 17th and 18th CENTURIES

In the 17th century, a mathematical revolution gripped Europe. Suddenly, working with INFINITY became all the rage, and a flurry of mathematicians tried to work out what Pi was all about.

For example, **John Wallis** (from England, 1616–1703) developed his very own formula to calculate Pi. He was also said to have come up with THIS COOL SYMBOL to describe infinity:

Swiss scientist **Leonhard Euler** (1707–1783) was not only a mathematician, he was also an astronomer, a physicist, a geographer and an engineer. Fancy that!

Like every mathematician ever, Leonhard was fascinated by Pi. He developed another pretty formula:

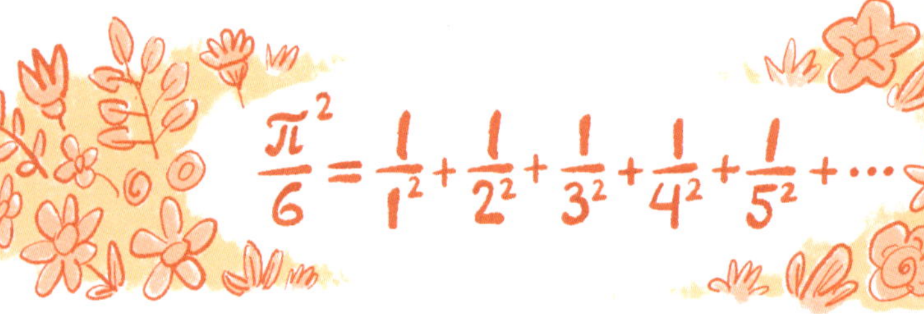


Now, all these formulas are very PRETTY and CLEVER, but there was a PROBLEM. None of them are actually very EFFICIENT. If you use them, it would take you a long time to work out even a small number of Pi's decimal places.

But luckily for the world, along came John Machin.

TADA!

**John Machin** (c.1686–1751) was an English astronomer. He was the first person EVER (or so we think!) to come up with a speedy formula for Pi. With it, he found the first 100 decimal places of Pi.

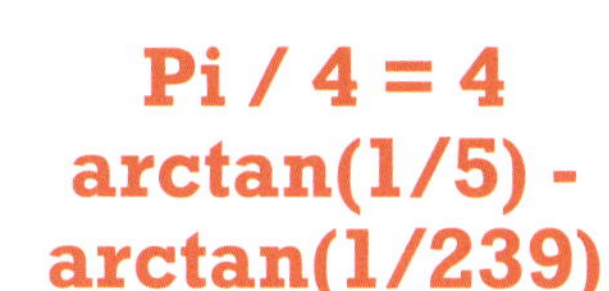


Pi / 4 = 4 arctan(1/5) - arctan(1/239)

For his formula, John used something nifty called arctangents.

Your best and wisest refuge from all troubles is in your science.

Arctangents are a bit of a beast to explain. Such a beast, in fact, that they would need a whole book to themselves.

**Ada Lovelace**
English mathematician
1815–1852

# JOHANN HEINRICH LAMBERT CRUSHES ALL HOPE

Until 1761, mathematicians everywhere still hoped that Pi was some kind of reasonable, RATIONAL number.
If Pi was rational, it would make everybody's life SO MUCH EASIER!

But no.
Pi did not play along.

In 1761, the Swiss–French mathematician **Johann Heinrich Lambert** (1728–1777) PROVED that Pi was irrational.

Johann Heinrich's family were poor. He had to leave school at age twelve to help in his dad's tailor shop. But J.H. REALLY WANTED TO STUDY MATH. So, he worked as a tutor for rich families. This way, he got to read lots of books!

Among many other things, he proved beyond a doubt that Pi is an irrational number: infinite and non-repeating. Johann Heinrich now knew for sure that no one would EVER get to the bottom of Pi.
We don't know if Johann Heinrich was sad about his discovery. Maybe he was EXCITED, because finding an irrational number is surely
SO
MUCH
MORE
EXCITING
than a well-behaved, rational one!
Now that everyone agreed that Pi was irrational, mathematicians went into a PI FRENZY. They all wanted to calculate as many of Pi's decimal places as possible.

# PEAK GEEK TIME: 19th CENTURY

## ZACHARIAS DAHSE AND HIS INCREDIBLE BRAIN

**Johann Martin Zacharias Dahse** (1824–1861, from Hamburg, Germany) had an incredible talent for numbers. He could tell you exactly how many books there were in a library with one look. Without counting, he knew how many sheep there were in a flock, and could tell you the exact sum of a game of dominoes with one glance.

Audiences around Europe went MAD for Zacharias Dahse's amazing brain, and in 1844 he decided to use it to calculate as many of Pi's decimal places as he could! He did this mostly in his head, without paper or pencil. In just TWO MONTHS he'd worked out 200 decimal places—a new record!

# WILLIAM SHANKS, THE MAN WHO MADE ONLY ONE MISTAKE ...

Imagine being so in love with Pi that you spend most of your life working on it!

**William Shanks** (1812–1882, from England) spent DECADES finding as many decimal places as he could. Every morning, he got up and did his calculations, and every afternoon he went over the morning's work, to check for errors.

In the course of his life, William worked out a whopping 707 decimal places!

Now this would be a lovely story, EXCEPT ... At the 528th decimal place, William made a **MISTAKE.** And he didn't notice it.

(This just goes to show that mistakes happen to even the most careful people.) For TEN YEARS, William continued his calculations—WITH THE MISTAKE! He never found out and died a happy man. And for the next 70 years, no one else noticed, either!

# THE PI ROOM

In 1937, the good people of Paris built a CIRCULAR room JUST FOR PI: the Pi Room. It included all of Pi's 707 known decimal places—as calculated by William Shanks.

Seven years after the Pi Room opened, mathematician D.F. Ferguson used one of the first calculating machines and discovered William's mistake!

So, in 1949, all the incorrect digits from no. 527 onwards were removed and replaced with the RIGHT ones.

So, when YOU go and visit the Pi Room at the Palace of Discovery in Paris, you can be assured that the digits are **ALL CORRECT.**

# SRINIVASA RAMANUJAN DREAMS OF MATH

Godfrey Harold Hardy (1877–1947), from Britain, was a distinguished mathematics professor at Cambridge University.

One day in 1913, he received a thick letter from India. In it, he found over 120 formulas ...

... that just about cracked up his brain– because they were so

One of the formulas is the most efficient way to calculate the number Pi that we have ever seen ...

The sender of the letter was **Srinivasa Ramanujan** (1887–1920) from Chennai, India.

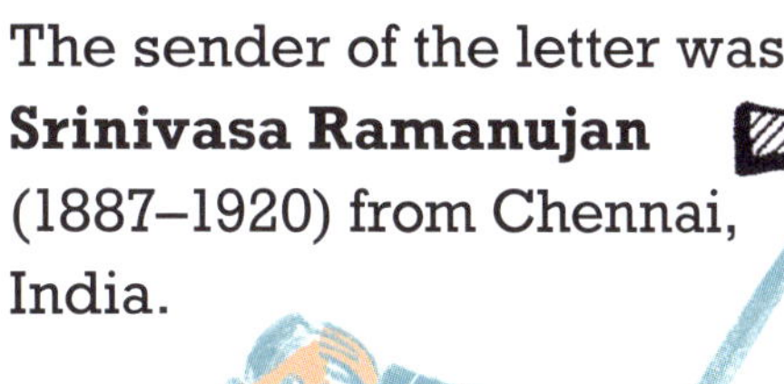

Srinivasa was only interested in math, and nothing else. He refused to work on any other subjects ... so, he failed school!

Instead, he mainly taught himself, and filled pages and pages of notebooks with formulas.

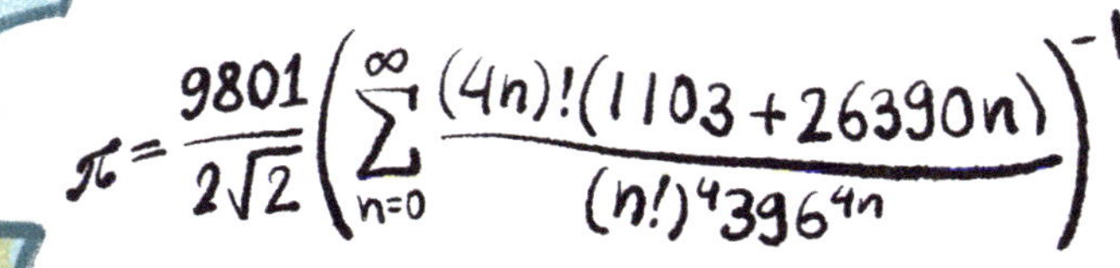


Srinivasa developed his first theorem when he was just thirteen years old. He said that the formulas came to him, fully formed, in his dreams.

**A theorem** is a statement that can be proven to be true.

Srinivasa developed dozens of different formulas to calculate Pi's decimals.
Some of these formulas were entirely new to the world. He even found a formula that, instead of just one, reveals eight decimal places at a time!
What a beauty!
The English mathematicians were sceptical of Srinivasa's work. They wanted to see METHOD and PROOF, and Srinivasa didn't offer this.
"Formulas from DREAMS?"
the mathematicians at Cambridge said to each other, shaking their heads.
"Whatever next?"
So, instead of being incredibly IMPRESSED that someone could produce such amazing work
just from their DREAMS,
they laughed at Srinivasa.

**Srinivasa Ramanujan**
Indian mathematician
1887–1920

# COMPUTERS TAKE OVER: 20th and 21st CENTURIES

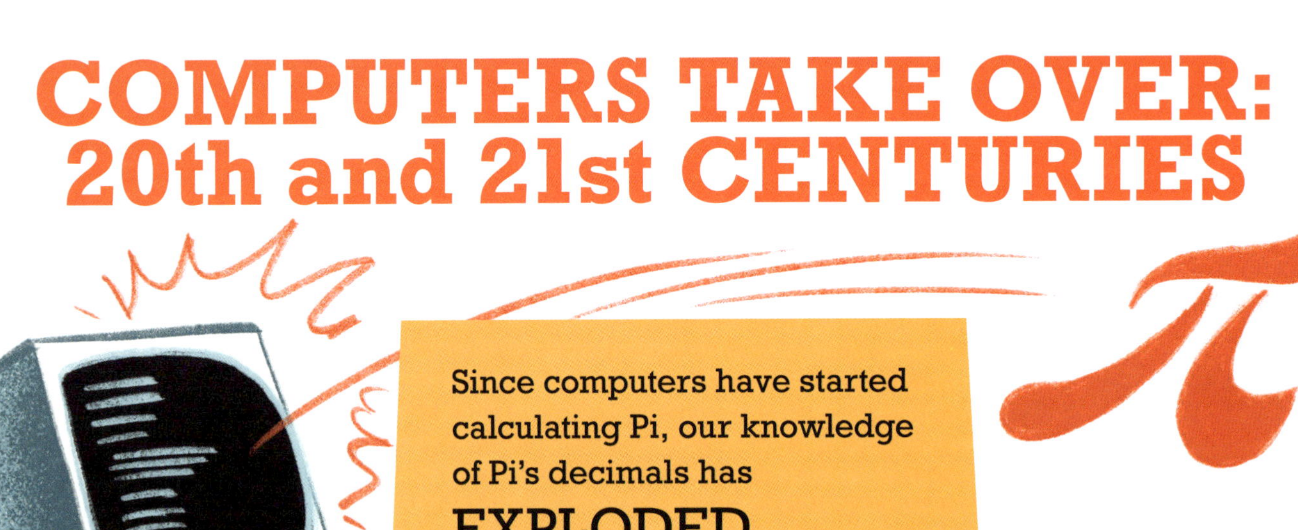

Since computers have started calculating Pi, our knowledge of Pi's decimals has **EXPLODED.**

In 1945, we knew 527 decimal places. It took thousands of years to get there. And now, just 80 years later, here we are at over 100 TRILLION decimal places! This means that humanity has gone from finding one decimal place every ten years to over one billion ... every day!

It's nice to have machines to help us with heavy calculations. However, the formulas that the machines use still come from humans—some of them straight from Srinivasa Ramanujan.

**Fun fact: Simon Plouffe** (born 1956 in Québec, Canada) developed a way to calculate the numbers in Pi without even knowing the numbers that come before, using a binary system. Extraordinary!

# TWO TIMES TWO BROTHERS ...

In the 1990s, the **BORWEIN brothers** from Scotland proved that Srinivasa Ramanujan's formula was correct. They worked on the original formula to make it even more efficient.

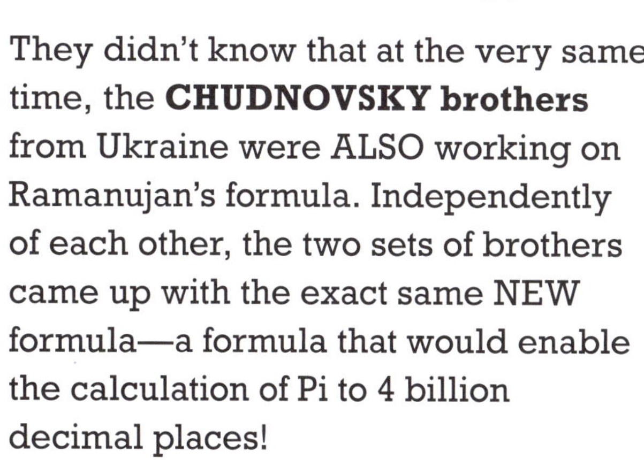

They didn't know that at the very same time, the **CHUDNOVSKY brothers** from Ukraine were ALSO working on Ramanujan's formula. Independently of each other, the two sets of brothers came up with the exact same NEW formula—a formula that would enable the calculation of Pi to 4 billion decimal places!

Why is Pi so lucky in love? Because its love is infinite and non-repeating.

**Fun fact:** In 2016, **Emma Haruka Iwao** (born in 1986 in Tokyo, Japan) led her team to set the Guinness World Record for calculating over 31 trillion of Pi's digits.

But that wasn't enough for Emma. In 2022, she BROKE HER OWN RECORD—with 100 trillion digits!

# THE QUESTION IS: WHY?

What even is the POINT of knowing all these decimals for Pi?
Well, some people are obsessed with fashion. Others are fascinated by words. And some are obsessed with Pi and its decimals.

Each to their own!

It's true that we don't really NEED to know very many decimal places to use Pi for precise calculations. Even to send a spacecraft to the moon, NASA (the American space agency) only ever used the first 15 decimals of Pi ...

But Pi decimals ARE sometimes useful!

## TESTING COMPUTERS!

How do you know whether the supercomputer you've just made is any good? Well, you ask it to find Pi's decimals. This is an excellent test to see whether the computer is functioning properly.

IBM 590, for example, FAILED that test when it was developed, so it got binned!

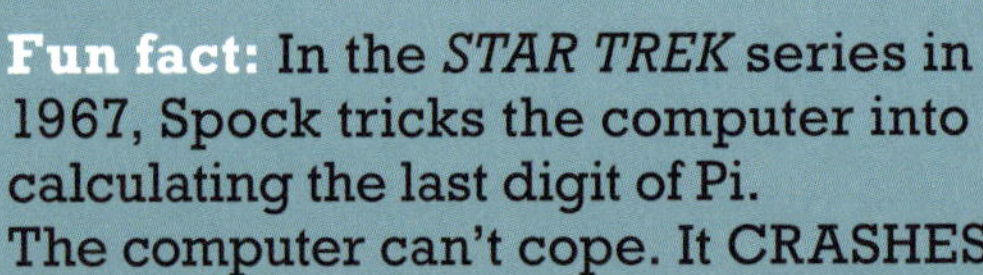

**Fun fact:** In the *STAR TREK* series in 1967, Spock tricks the computer into calculating the last digit of Pi.
The computer can't cope. It CRASHES.

# AS GOOD AS RANDOM ...

Today, we know trillions of decimal places for Pi. And because Pi is IRRATIONAL, its decimals look pretty

RANDOM to us ...

(Please note: Pi is NOT a RANDOM number! But nobody will ever find a pattern in Pi, so to us humans, Pi's decimals are as close to randomness as we might ever get ...)

Our human brains are not good at generating or recognizing randomness. This is because they have "cognitive bias." But sometimes we need to come up with a random number sequence. So, the decimals of Pi seem like a pretty good way to pretend.

**Maryam Mirzakhani**
Iranian mathematician
1977–2017

**Cognitive bias** is a type of thinking error people can make when they are processing information and are influenced by things they already know.

Pi has become a math superstar. It's like a celebrity! Pi is so famous that nearly everyone in the world has at least heard of it. Your teacher might even have talked about Pi at school (but maybe you were very busy picking your nose, so you can't quite remember).

**Fun fact: Pi Day** is celebrated around the world every year on March 14 (i.e., 3.14. Geddit?). It's a great way to connect with other mathematicians, to exchange knowledge and to geek out on Pi. There is even an official website where you can find jokes, riddles and other fun Pi-related activities: piday.org.

# WE'VE COME FULL CIRCLE!

So thousands upon thousands of BRILLIANT MINDS have thought about PI and STUDIED PI and INVESTIGATED PI and computers now know how to calculate **TRILLIONS** of its decimals ...

Given that Pi has kept humanity busy for thousands of years, you'd think that, by now, we would know a lot about it, right?

**RIGHT?**

How much does humanity know about PI TODAY? Turn the page to find out!

What humanity
knows about Pi
today.

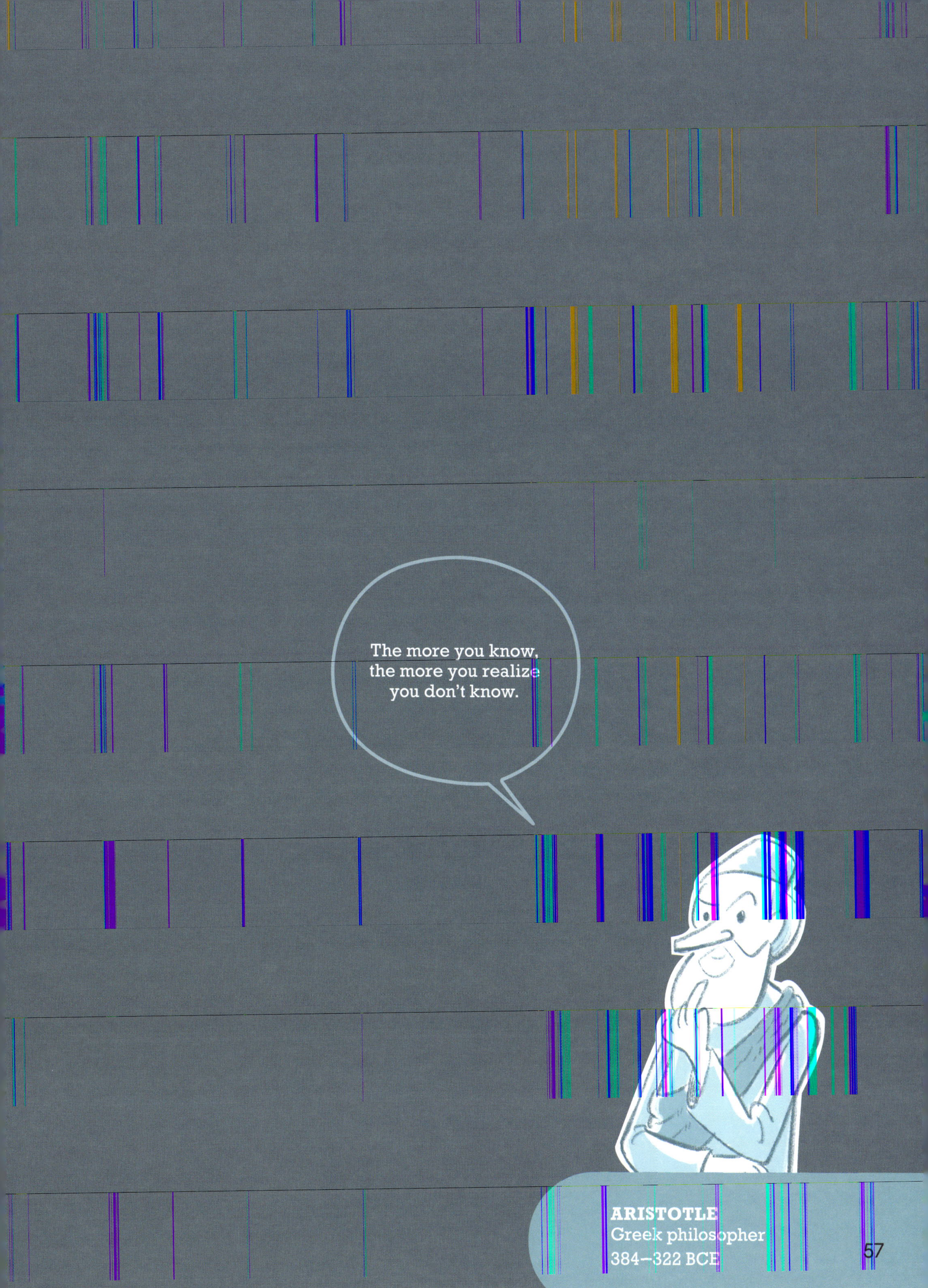
The more you know, the more you realize you don't know.
ARISTOTLE
Greek philosopher
384–322 BCE

But do not despair! Even though we know next to NOTHING, and even though Pi stubbornly remains a MYSTERY and turns up in the most UNEXPECTED places, we can still

**USE PI**

and work with it.

It's **EXTREMELY USEFUL**, for example, when you need to impress your friends with magic tricks, your incredible memory, or your pizza-cutting skills.

That's what we'll look at in the next chapter.

**Fun fact:** You could spend your entire life reciting trillions of decimals of Pi, and you'd still only ever get to … 0% of the decimals in PI …

CHAPTER 3.1415
FUN WITH PI
BEWARE!!! If you do not want to THINK, then this chapter is DEFINITELY. NOT. FOR. YOU.
It's not for the FAINT OF HEART, nor the WOBBLY OF MIND.
It's for those who
WANT TO KNOW (and then go and impress all their friends).
ARE YOU ONE OF THEM?
IS YOUR BRAIN BRAINING?
ARE YOU READY?

# MEMORIZING PI DIGITS

People LOVE Pi and some spend YEARS learning its decimals by heart.

**Julia Rozenkova** from Australia was just five years old when she recited Pi to its 200th decimal place in 2016!

**Suresh Kumar Sharma**, a vegetable farmer from India, beat the official world record in 2015, having memorized 70,030 digits of Pi. It took him over 17 hours to recite them all!

It took six-year-old **Ishani Shanmugam** (born 2015) only ten minutes to recite 1560 decimal places for Pi—which made her the Singapore Book of Records holder in 2021.

**Akira Haraguchi** (born 1946) is a retired engineer from Japan. He holds the current unofficial world record for Pi, having recited 100,000 digits in 16 hours. "Unofficial" because the Guinness World Records have not accepted this record yet—despite Akira's best efforts to prove that he didn't cheat. He was recorded the entire time—even when he went to the toilet!

What about you? How many digits of Pi do you know by heart?

# TRAIN YOUR BRAIN TO MEMORIZE PI

One nifty trick to learn Pi's decimals is to use something called **MNEMONICS.**

*"How I wish I could enumerate Pi easily, since all these horrible mnemonics prevent recalling any of Pi's sequences more simply."*

What a mouthful!

Each word in *that sentence* has the number of letters that corresponds to the digits in Pi.

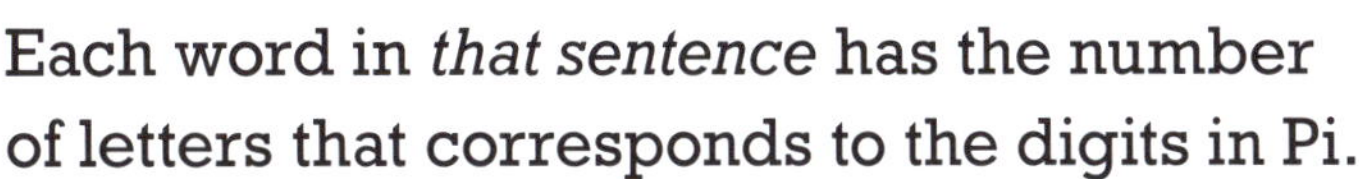

H-o-w: 3 letters

I: 1 letter

w-i-s-h: 4 letters

(i.e., 3.14 …)

… and so on!

See how many digits you can learn by heart with this method!

Reserve your right to think. For even to think wrongly is better than not to think at all.

**Hypatia of Alexandria**
Egyptian mathematician
c.360–415 CE

# PI CAN! CAN YOU?

Look at this soda can.
Which do you think is longer:
its circumference or height?

Chances are, you will think that the height of the can is greater than its circumference.

**BUT … IS THAT RIGHT?**

No, it's not right at all!

To calculate the circumference, we simply multiply the diameter by Pi. This gives us ca. 2.07 ... which is waaaayyy longer than the can's height. Almost double, in fact!

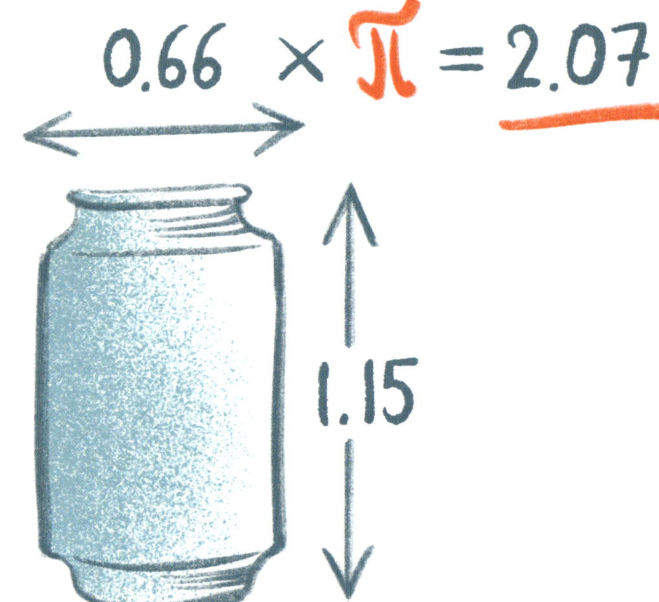

This becomes even more impressive when you try it with a sleek can.

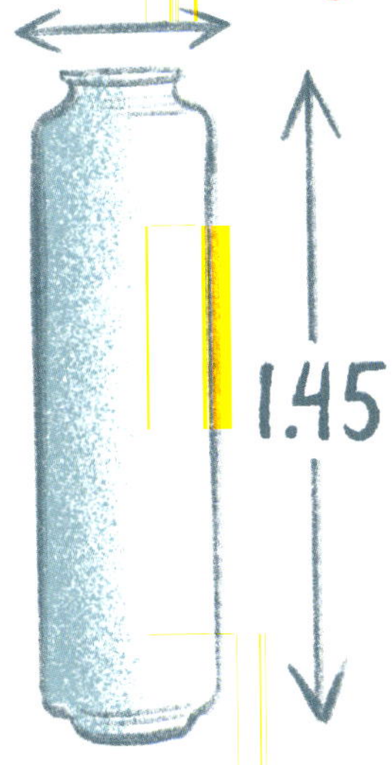


1.972 is bigger than 1.45!

So even with a slimline can, the circumference is longer than the height!

## BUT ... WHY ISN'T THAT JUST OBVIOUS?

It's an optical illusion. Our brain finds it tricky to "unroll" a circumference in space to estimate its real length, and we get FOOLED into thinking that the circumference is smaller than it really is.

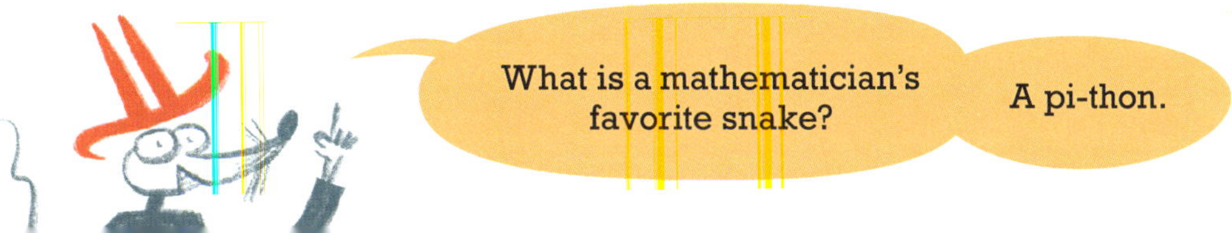

What is a mathematician's favorite snake?

A pi-thon.

# PI PARADOXES

Here is a paradox to
**MELT YOUR BRAIN.**

Why shouldn't you eat too much Pi? Because you'll end up with a big circumference!

Let's take the Earth, and let's assume that it's perfectly round. (In reality it isn't perfectly round, of course. True perfection only really exists in mathematicians' heads!)

Now we take a BELT and wrap it all the way around Earth's perfectly round tummy.

That belt's length would be exactly the circumference of the Earth.

**Right?**

But that belt is too TIGHT! Earth isn't quite comfortable. So, let's loosen it up a tiny bit.

We add
**ONE METER**
of length to the belt.

Now, the belt detaches itself a little from Earth's tummy ...

**A paradox** is an idea or statement that seems wrong and impossible, but at the same time makes sense. Paradoxes are confusing!

**The Swiss Cheese Paradox**
Swiss Emmental cheese has lots of holes. The more cheese you have, the more holes you have. The more holes you have, the less cheese you have. Thus, the more cheese you have, the less cheese you have. HUH?

The question is: BY HOW MUCH?

By how much does the belt detach itself from the Earth? How much space is now between Earth's tummy and the belt? What would you guess?

**Let's see!**

So, the circumference of the Earth is **40,000 km***. That is **40,000,000 m.** Now we add **1** meter to these **40,000,000 m.** Almost nothing!

Even so, adding this tiny amount detaches the belt by ... **16 cm**!

That seems a bit crazy, right? And that's why it is a

**PARADOX!**

16 cm

1m

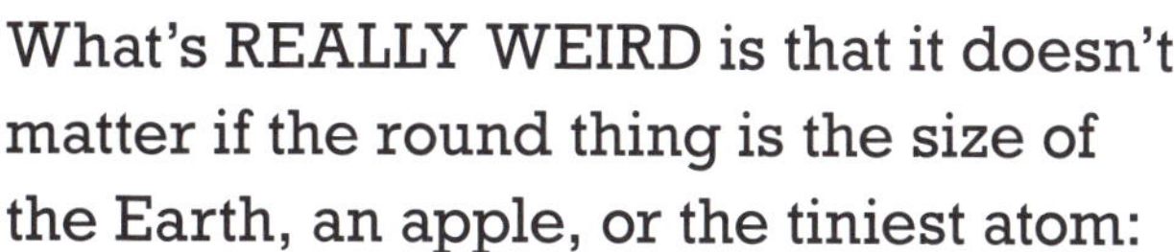

What's REALLY WEIRD is that it doesn't matter if the round thing is the size of the Earth, an apple, or the tiniest atom:

If you add **1 m** to any circle's circumference, the distance gained will ALWAYS be **16 cm.**

**Fancy that!**

*Of course that's not the EXACT circumference of the Earth, but let's keep it simple for our poor brains, shall we?

# Pi = 4.
# WAIT, WHAT?!

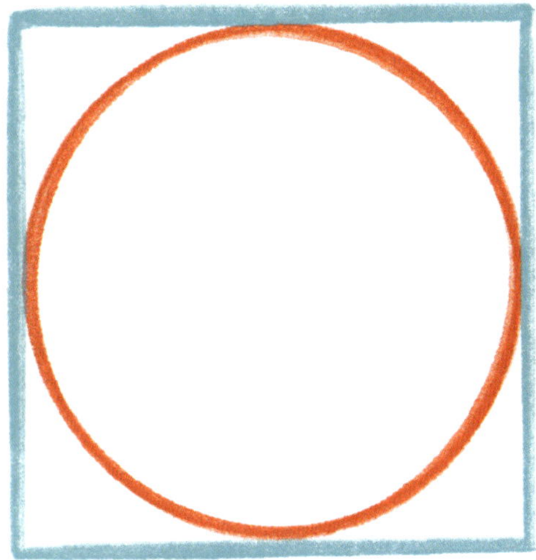

Here is a circle sitting right inside a square with a side measuring 1. So, of course, the circle's diameter is 1 and its circumference is Pi. And the square's perimeter is **4 (1+1+1+1).**

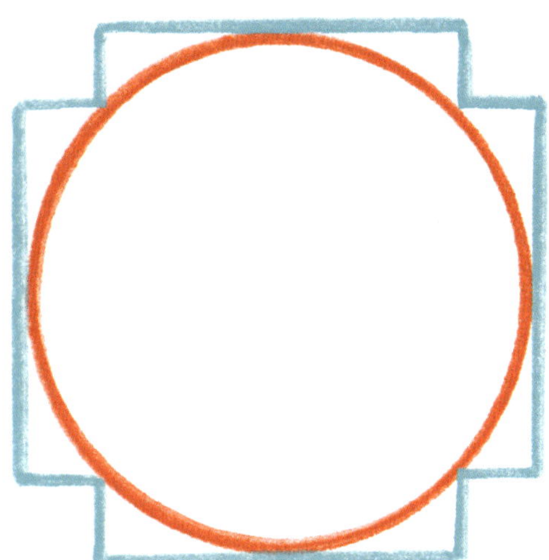

Now we take away a small square from each corner of the big square. Does this change the perimeter of the outside shape? NO, IT DOES NOT. The perimeter is still **4**. Right?

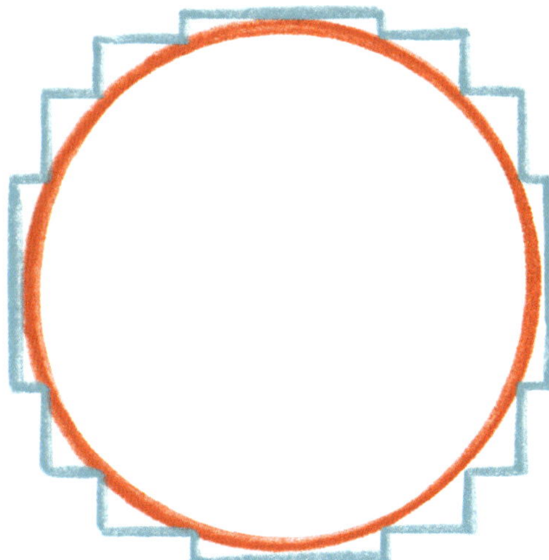

Let's keep cutting squares out of the first big square.
The perimeter is **STILL 4**. BUT ... we're getting closer to the shape of the circle ...

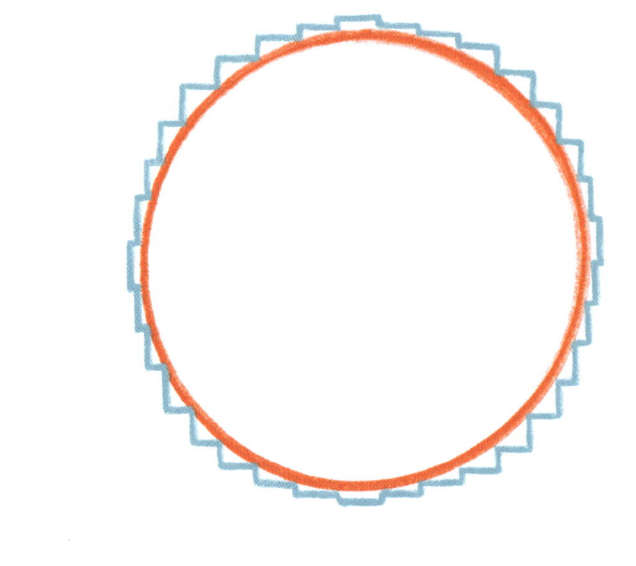

If we cut into the outside shape an INFINITE number of times, the line of the circle and the line of the perimeter will look

ALMOST THE SAME.

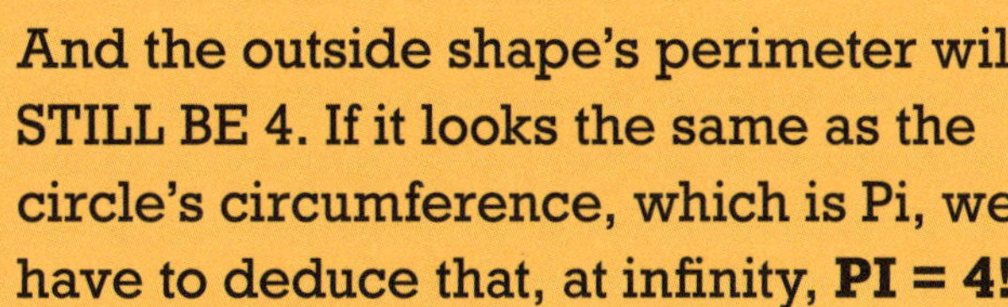

And the outside shape's perimeter will STILL BE 4. If it looks the same as the circle's circumference, which is Pi, we have to deduce that, at infinity, **PI = 4!**

This isn't true, of course. The perimeter just LOOKS like it might become the same as the circumference at some infinite point, but it never will. What a paradox!

What's wrong with the equation Pi r squared? Pi are round. Cake are square.

## Pi = 2.
## What, what, WHAT??

So, just before, we said Pi = 4, and now we're saying Pi = 2?

Let's look at this cool

**PARADOX.**

For this, you need to understand the following:

**The length of a semicircle with a diameter of 2 equals ...**

**the length of a circle with a diameter of 1.**

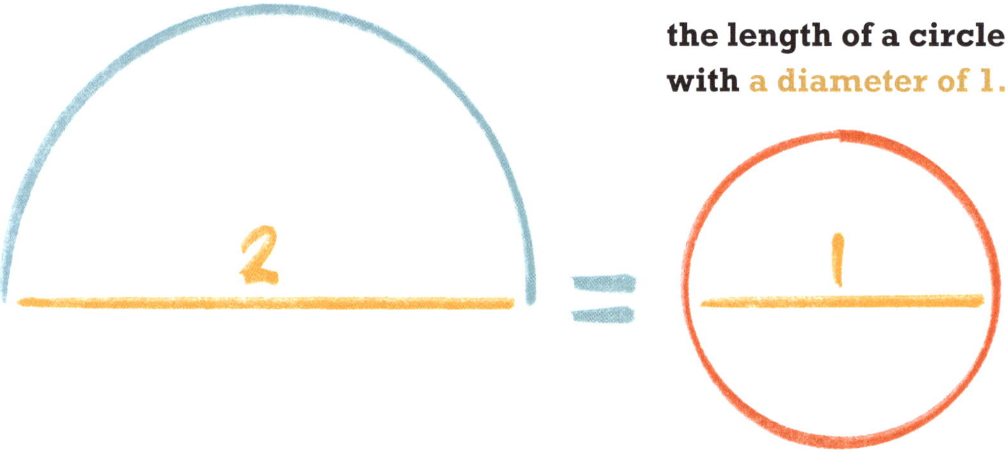

$2 = 1$

Or in other words (erm ... pictures):

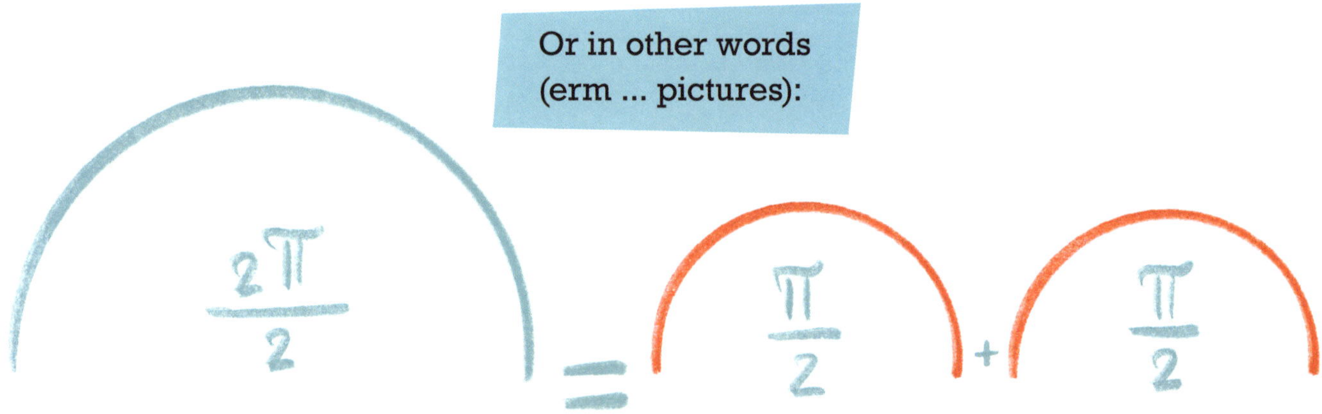

$\frac{2\pi}{2} = \frac{\pi}{2} + \frac{\pi}{2}$

**The radius** is half of a diameter.

**A semicircle** is half a circle.

Whether one larger semicircle or two smaller ones, the combined length remains Pi.

Right?

Here is a blue semicircle. Let's break it up! The red and blue shape are the same length: Pi.

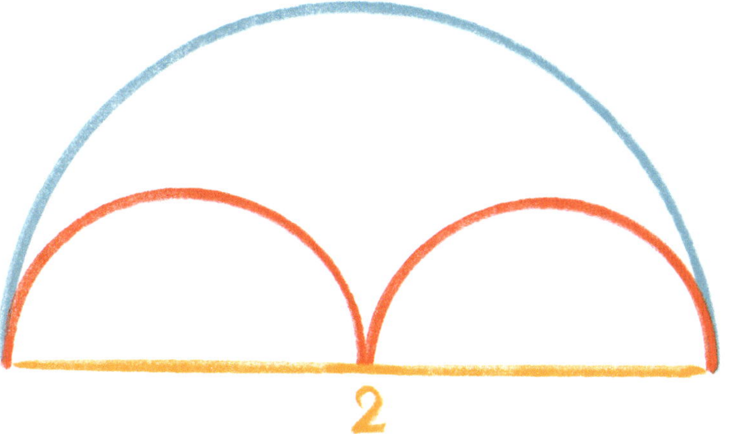


Let's break it up again to make four semicircles!

This shape has the same length as the others. It's still the length of Pi.

Now, we make eight semicircles.

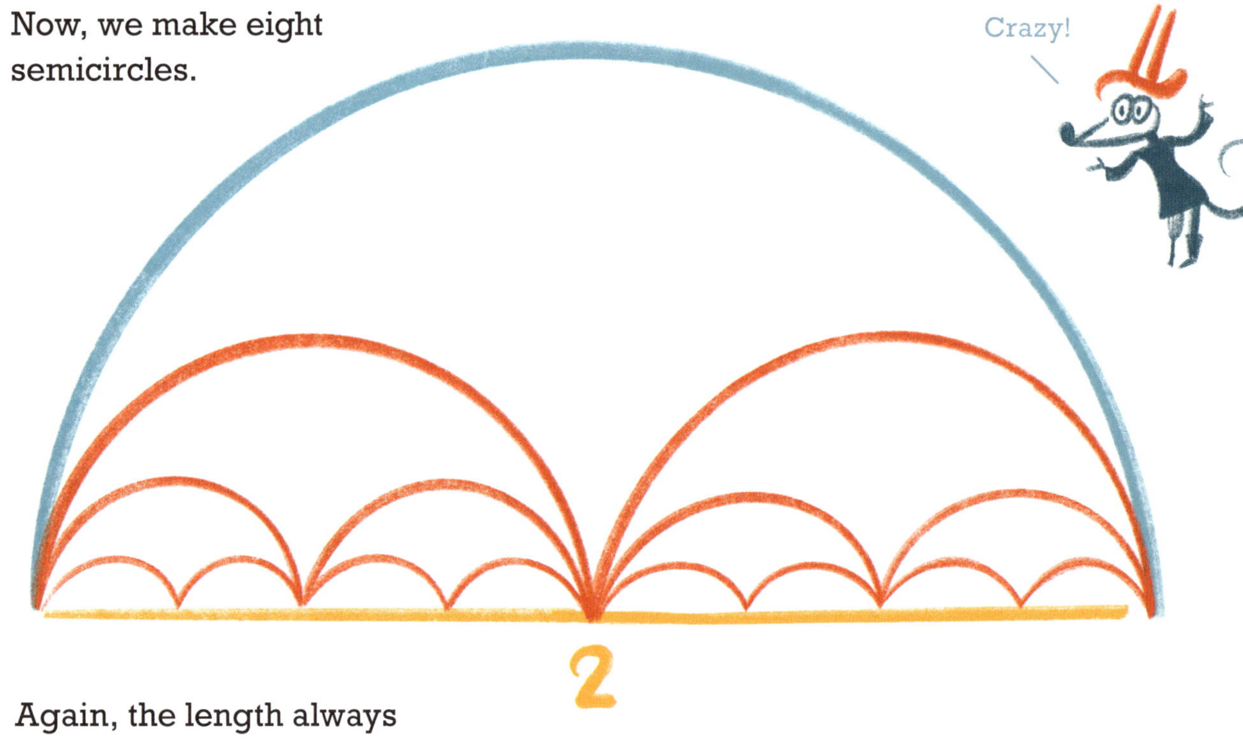


Again, the length always remains the same: Pi.

And now do this again and again and again.

2

Crazier ... and outrageous!

No matter how many times you break up the shape, its length never changes.

If you do this an INFINITE number of times, the semicircle line and the diameter start converging: it looks like they become one and the same …

2

Which would mean that, at infinity, Pi = 2!

**SO.**

**Pi = 2** and then **Pi = 4.**
So … **4 = 2. And then 1 = 2.**

**OH DEAR.**

Our brains can get very confused when working with infinity! So:

**HANDLE INFINITY WITH CARE!**

Infinity is infinitely fascinating.

# HOW TO CUT A PIZZA ...

## 1. INTO 3 EQUAL SLICES

You will need:
**A pizza**
**A piece of string**
**3 people who are equally hungry**

Did you know that the volume of a pizza of height A and radius of Z is equal to PI ZZ A?

**1.** Stretch the string across the middle of the pizza to get its diameter.

**2.** Cut the string. It is now exactly the length of the diameter.

**3.** The pizza's circumference is 3.14 times the length of the diameter—just over 3.

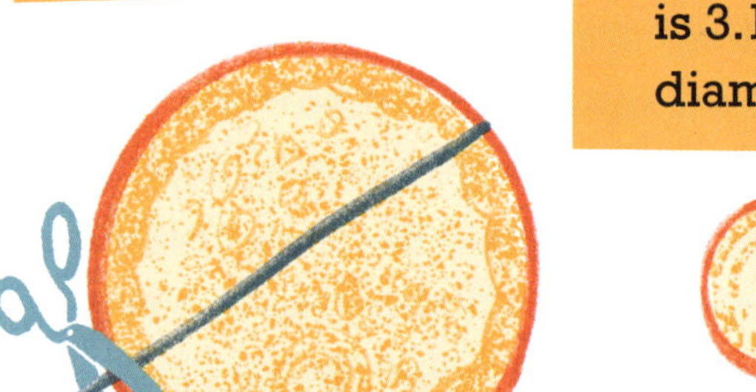

**4.** So, to get 3 (almost) equal pieces, you simply place your string along the circumference of the pizza, and mark where to cut.

**5.** Do this 3 times.

**6.** Cut your pizza into 3 equal slices.

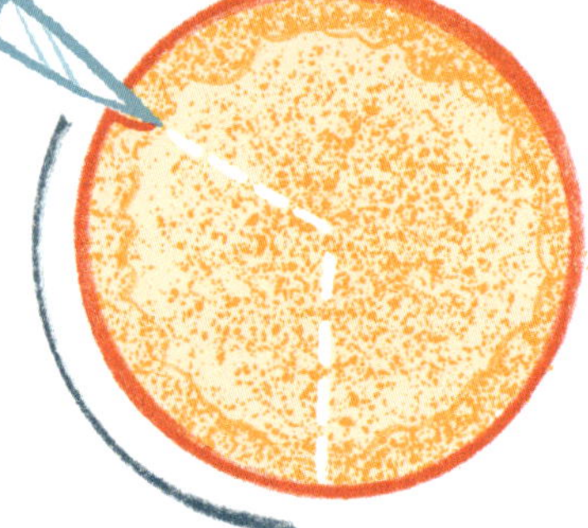

**7.** Enjoy your pizza.

## 2. IN HALF

OK so now you only have to share the pizza between two of you.

**BUT!**

One of you really loves the CRUST. And the other one only likes the SOGGY BIT in the middle.
You both want a fair share.

OH NO! WHAT TO DO NOW???

You need:
**A pizza**
**A tape measure**
**2 people to eat the pizza**

**1.** Measure the DIAMETER of the pizza.

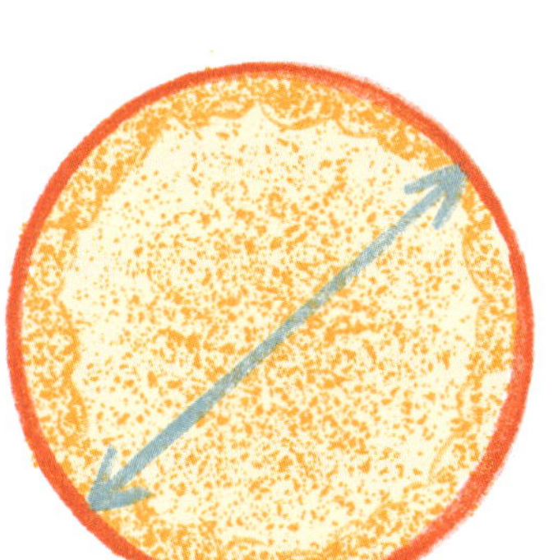

**2.** Divide this number by 8.

**3.** Now measure this number from the outside rim of the pizza. Mark the spot.

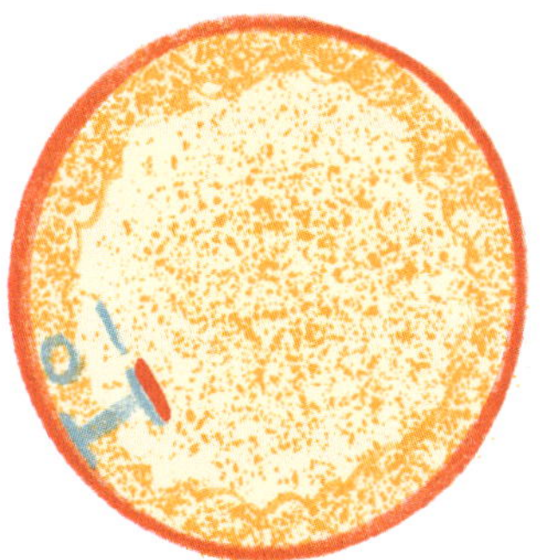

**4.** Do the same thing a few times around the pizza. The more places you mark, the more precise your circle will be!

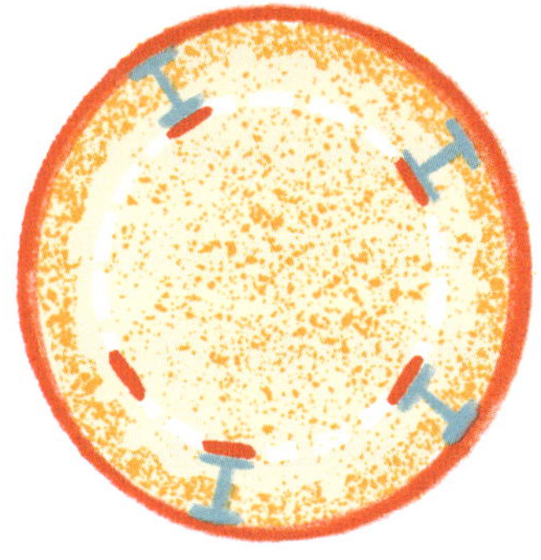

**5.** Cut along the marks.

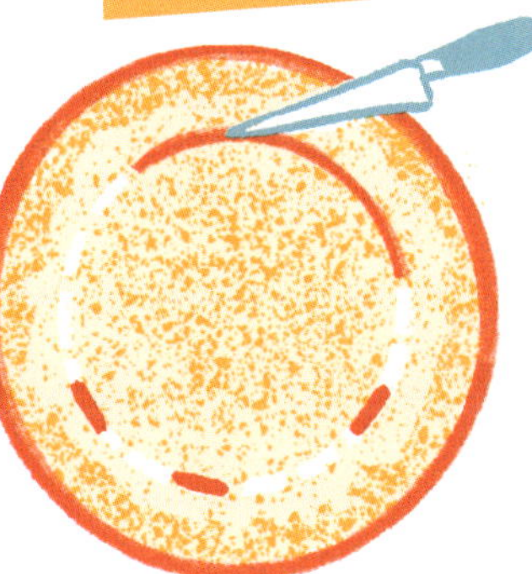

**6.** Congratulations! Enjoy your pizza!

**7.** Wash your tape measure before the tomato sauce dries.

**8.** Don't tell your parents you used a tape measure on a pizza.

# FISH V. BIRD: IT'S SO UNFAIR!

It turns out that Pi also turns up when measuring the length of RIVERS.

**FANCY THAT!**

A FISH and a BIRD meet at the source of a river.

Let's race all the way to the sea!

If they go at exactly the same speed, who will win? The bird or the fish? The BIRD, of course, because it can fly STRAIGHT. The fish has to swim along the river's meanders.

**TALK ABOUT UNFAIR ADVANTAGE!**

So, the fish has to go further ... But by how much?

And this is where Pi comes along ...

Let's look at this river: its meanders basically form

**SEMICIRCLES.**

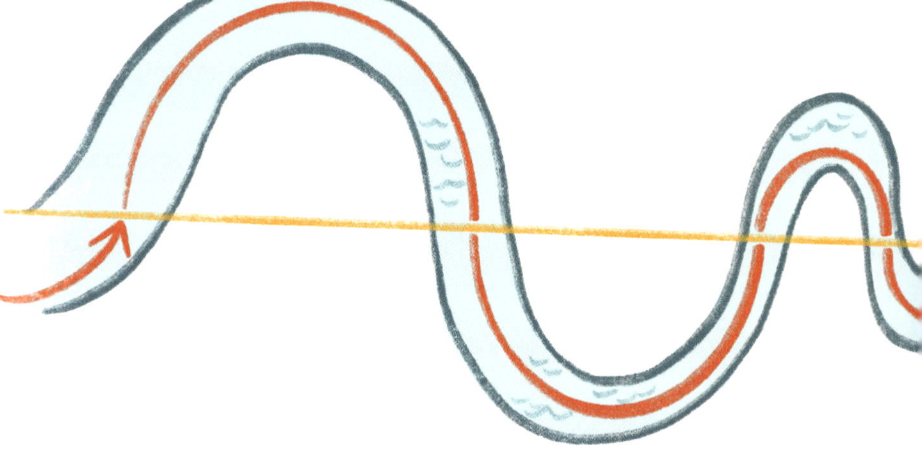

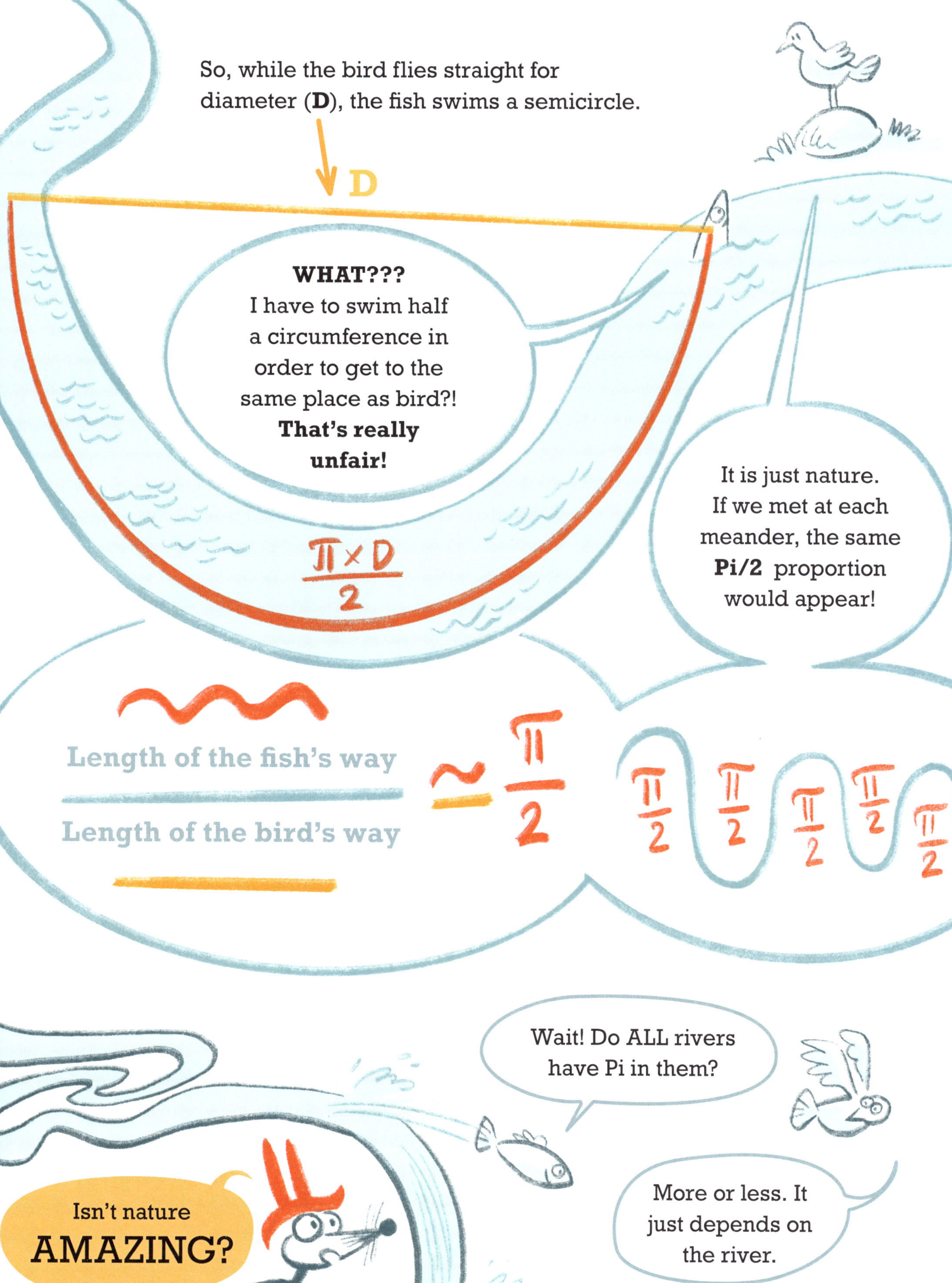
So, while the bird flies straight for diameter (**D**), the fish swims a semicircle.
D
**WHAT???**
I have to swim half a circumference in order to get to the same place as bird?!
**That's really unfair!**
$\frac{\pi \times D}{2}$
It is just nature. If we met at each meander, the same **Pi/2** proportion would appear!
Length of the fish's way
Length of the bird's way
$\simeq \frac{\pi}{2}$
$\frac{\pi}{2}$ $\frac{\pi}{2}$ $\frac{\pi}{2}$ $\frac{\pi}{2}$ $\frac{\pi}{2}$
Wait! Do ALL rivers have Pi in them?
More or less. It just depends on the river.
Isn't nature AMAZING?

# A PI-LICIOUS MAGIC TRICK

All dates are linked to Pi!

Give me a date, any date, for example your date of birth.

The date needs to be in the following format:
**dd mm yyyy.**

June 4, 2016
=

**04062016**

Then, enter this number into a calculator with a point after the first digit (which may well be 0).

***0.4062016***

Now multiply the number you have entered by exactly 6.2831853, and see what the result is.

***0.4062016***
***x***
***6.2831853***
***=***
***2.5522399***

At this point, the magician needs to do a little bit of math.

I need to calculate the initial number given by the audience **times 2.**

**2**
**x**
**0.4062016**
**=**
**0.8124032**

Now I pretend to think very hard.
2.5522399 / 0.8124032 =
Divide your result by 0.8124032.
And, as if by magic, the result is:
3.14159265!
Pi to a precision of seven digits: Archimedes would be jealous!
You can use any date you like and try it out for yourself: d.dmmyyyy x 6.2831853 / (2 x d.dmmyyyy) and the result is ... 3.14159265.
The trick behind this mindblowing little trick is that 6.2831853 ≈ 2π.
So, the formula for this trick always goes like this: 2π ½ = π!

# CHAPTER 3.14159

# JOKES

Why did Pi fail its driving test?

Because it didn't know when to stop.

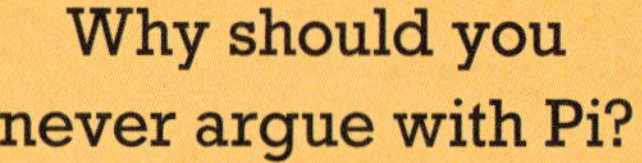

Why should you never argue with Pi?

Because it's completely irrational.

Why was the math book so sad?

Because it had so many problems.

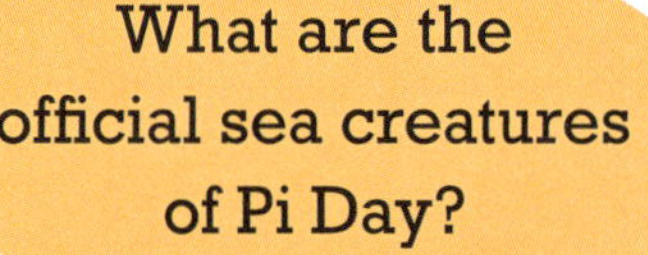

What are the official sea creatures of Pi Day?

Octopi.

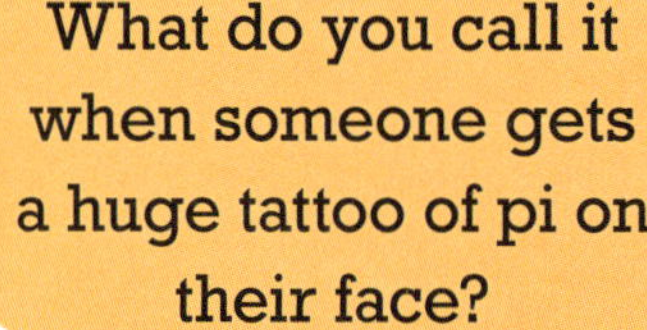

What do you call it when someone gets a huge tattoo of pi on their face?

An irrational decision.

How many bakers does it take to bake a pi?
3.14
Why did the triangle feel sorry for the circle?
Because it's pointless . . .
What did Pi say when someone asked if it could explain what Pi Day was again?
"I don't want to repeat myself."
Why did the mathematician become a secret agent?
She wanted to be a s-pi!
What do you get when a bunch of sheep stand around in a circle?
Shepherd's Pi.

# CHAPTER 3.141592

# E-PI-LOGUE

Pi is an extraordinary number.

It shows up in so many areas of our lives: geometry, probability, number theory, hydrology, astronomy, quantum physics, and more.

But at the same time, Pi is not an extraordinary number at all. That is because almost ALL numbers out there are IRRATIONAL, just like Pi—we just don't know very much about them! Humans only really stumbled over Pi because of its relationship to circles.

Our knowledge about Pi is extremely limited, just like our knowledge about most things. Almost everything remains to be explored further in this fascinating world of ours!

So, remain open and curious about the world, friends. And never stop asking questions.

Anita, Jean-Baptiste, Joonas,
Little Horsey PiPi, and Pi-Rat

**Pliny the Elder**
Roman author and philosopher
23–79 CE

# CHAPTER 3.1415926

# PROVE IT!

Here, you will find the calculations behind some of the statements in this book. You might find them interesting if you're really into math, but the authors will not be offended if you decide to skip this part.

## 1 The Egyptians' estimate for Pi (p. 26)

The ancient Egyptians noticed the following:

Area of [square with side 8] $\simeq$ Area of [circle with diameter 9]

$$64 \simeq \pi \times \left(\frac{9}{2}\right)^2 \quad *$$

$$\pi \simeq \frac{64}{\left(\frac{9}{2}\right)^2} = \frac{256}{81} \simeq 3.16$$

***Remember, the area of** [circle with radius r] $= \pi r^2$

## 2 Archimedes' calculations (p. 31)

Proof that Pi > 2.828 (perimeter of the square inside the circle)

**Length of** 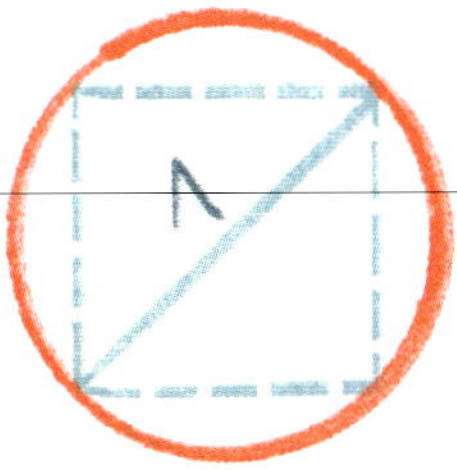

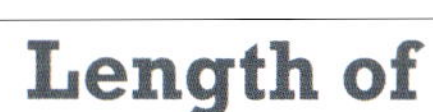

> **Length of** 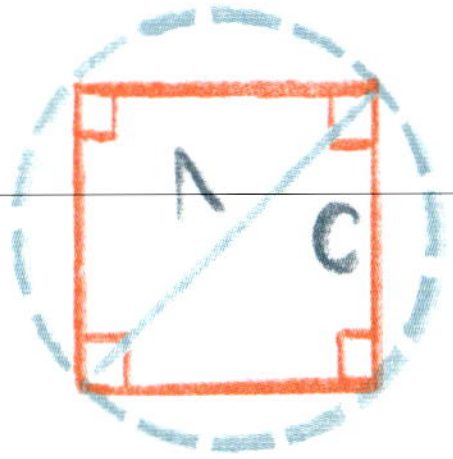


$$\pi > 4c$$

$c = ?$

$$c^2 + c^2 = 1^2 \,*$$

$$2c^2 = 1$$

$$c^2 = \frac{1}{2}$$

$$c = \frac{1}{\sqrt{2}} \,**$$

$$\pi > 4 \times \frac{1}{\sqrt{2}} = 2\sqrt{2} \simeq 2.828$$

***Pythagoras showed that if** 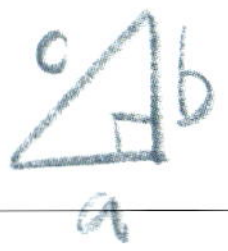

**, then** $a^2 + b^2 = c^2$

** $\sqrt{x}$ **: square root of x.**

## 3 What is calculus? (p. 38)

In volume VII of his encyclopedia, Jean-Baptiste Aubin—just kidding—Jean-Baptiste le Rond d'Alembert (France, 1717–1783) defined calculus as:

**"The new geometry of the infinitely small."**

**Calculus was used to study Pi.**

For example, Irishman William Brouncker (1620–1684) was both a musician and a mathematician. He developed this formula using calculus to work out Pi. It almost looks like a music score, doesn't it?

$$\frac{4}{\pi} = 1 + \cfrac{1^2}{2 + \cfrac{3^2}{2 + \cfrac{5^2}{2 + \cfrac{7^2}{2 + \cfrac{9^2}{2 + \dots}}}}}$$

## The Earth's belt paradox (p. 64–65)

**1) Initial Circumference:**

$C = 2\pi R$ **where** $R$ **is the Earth's radius.**

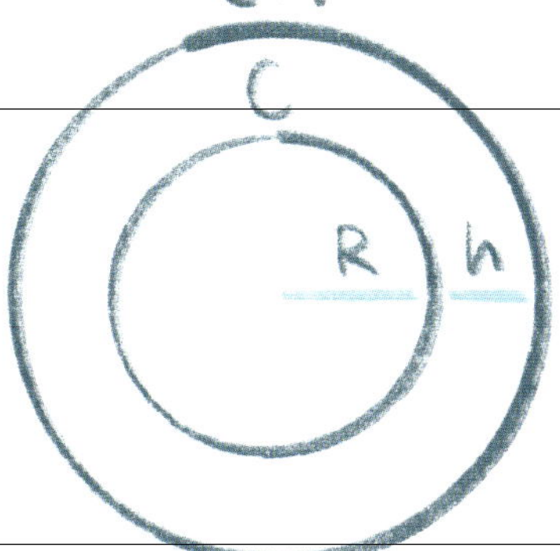


**2) New Circumference After Adding 1 Meter:**

$C' = C + 1 = 2\pi(R+h)$ **where** $h$ **is the uniform height at which the ribbon is lifted all around.**

**3) Solving for** $h$ **:**

$2\pi(R+h) = 2\pi R + 2\pi h = 2\pi R + 1$ **so** $2\pi h = 1$ **and then** $h = 1/2\pi$ **meters, in other words** $h = 0.16$ **meters.**

## How to cut a pizza (p. 73)

To get two equal halves of a pizza with a radius of 1 (and an area of Pi), we start by finding the radius R of the small circle. This way, we can check that the area of the small circle is exactly half of the pizza (Pi/2).

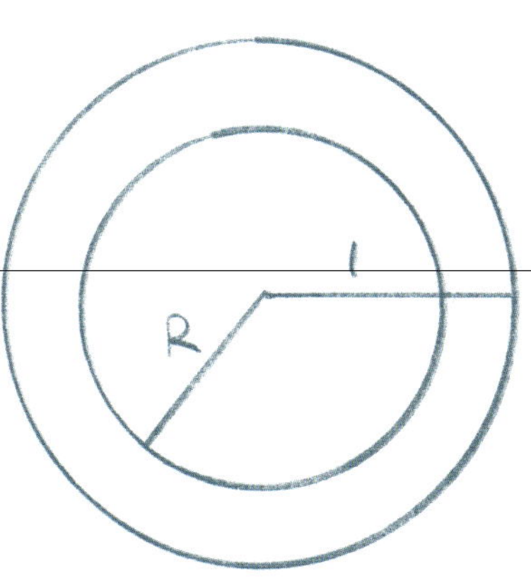


R is almost equal to ¾. So, you just need to take away 2/4 of the radius from the outside—i.e., 8/4 of the diameter—to give you two equal pieces.

$\pi \times R^2 = \frac{\pi}{2}$ **so,**

$R = \frac{1}{\sqrt{2}}$ **= ca. 3/4**

# CHAPTER 3.14159265

# GLOSSARY

**Algebra:** A branch of mathematics that deals with equations.

**Arctangent:** A mathematical tool based on the tangent to a circle.

**Binary system:** A system where numbers are written using only 1s and 0s.

**Circle:** A figure made up of all points that are at the same distance from a given point, called the center.

**Circumference:** The distance around the outside of a circle.

**Constant:** A value (or number) that does not change.

**Decimal:** A digit after the decimal point.

**Decimal number:** Decimal numbers help us write a number that is not a whole number (i.e., not 1, 2, 3, or 4, but something in between, like 1.23, 4.5 or 5.33333).

**Decimal place:** The position of the decimal number after the decimal point.

**Decimal point:** The dot to the left of a decimal, or between the decimal and whole number.

**Diameter:** The distance between two opposite points of a circle.

**Differential calculus:** A branch of mathematics where you can perform calculations with infinitely small quantities.

**Digit:** A figure in a number, e.g., the 3 in 3.14.

**Equation:** A "number sentence" that shows two things are equal (e.g., 2 + 7 = 9).

**Fraction:** Something that shows parts of a whole. Two examples of a fraction are ½ and ¼: one over two, or one half; and one over four, or one quarter.

**Geometry:** The branch of mathematics that studies shapes in space.

**Infinity:** Something that never ends.

**Irrational number:** A number that cannot be expressed as the ratio of two whole numbers.

**Number:** 1, 2, 3, and so on. There are two main families of numbers: rational numbers (decimals are periodic) and irrational numbers (decimals are infinite and aperiodic).

**Paradox:** An idea or statement that seems false and impossible, but at the same time makes sense.

**Perimeter:** The distance around the outside of a shape. Every shape has a perimeter. The perimeter of a circle, however, has a special name—the circumference.

**Periodic:** Something that forms a pattern that repeats, up to infinity.

**Polygon:** A shape that has more than three corners.

**Probability:** The branch of mathematics that deals with randomness.

**Radius:** Half of a diameter.

**Random:** Refers to something that depends on chance.

**Rational number:** A number that can be expressed as the ratio of two whole numbers. Interesting fact: A rational number's decimals are periodic, e.g., ½ and 3.15 are rationals. Pi isn't rational.

**Tangent:** A line that touches a circle and intersects it at only one point.

**Transcendental:** A sub-family of irrational numbers that includes Pi. We know very few transcendental numbers, but we know that it is the largest family of numbers! (Very confusing, we know!)

Room for more Pi? Download the Educator's Guide with additional Pi facts and challenges! Scan the QR code or go to:
https://hello.helvetiq.com/en-us/bigbookofpi

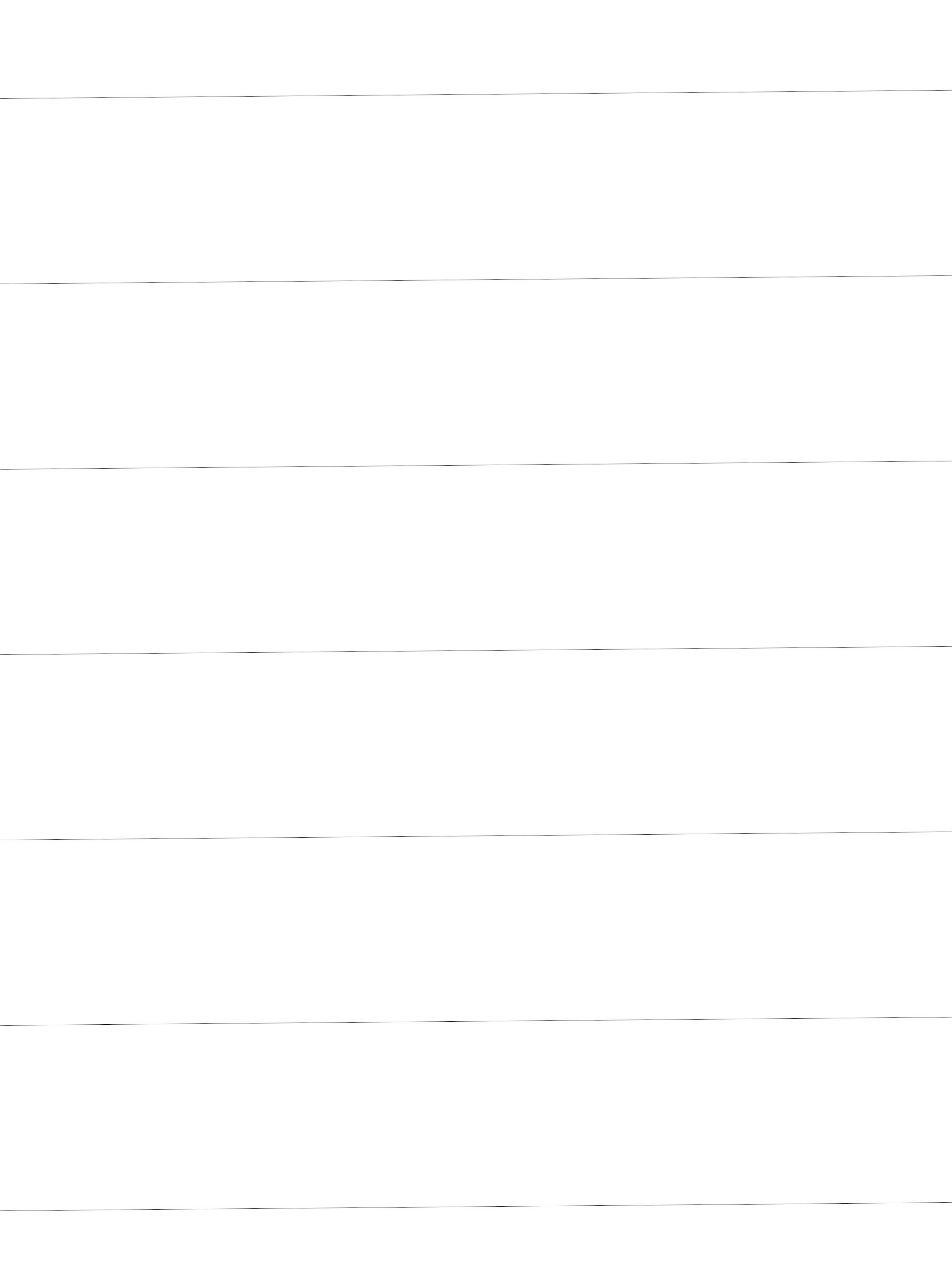

**...5840**0283624053460372634165542590276018348403068113818551059797056640075094260878857357960373245
2714943315155885403922164097229101129035521815762823283182342548326111912800928256190205263016391114
6369806637857681349204530224081972785647198396308781543221166912246415911776732253264335686146186545
2835257044133543758575342698699472547031656613991999682628247270641336222178923903176085428943733935
6703461491434478863604103182350736502778590897578272731305048893989009923913503373250855982655867089
7151058236267293264537382104938724996699339424685516483261134146110680267446637334375340764294026682
2506289058549145097157553900243931535190902107119457300243880176615035270862602537881797519478061013
8745649256443462392531953135103311476394911995072858430658361935369329699289837914941939406085724863
6218283025848112389011968221429457667580718653806506487026133892822994972574530332838963818439447707
1946334893748439129742391433659360410035234377706588867781139498616478747140793263858738624732889645
4464094758280348769758948328241239292960582948619196670918958089833201210318430340128495116203534280
4191102634163157147406123850425845988419907611287258059113935689601431668283176323567325417073420817
5337183868265617862273637169757741830239860065914816164049449650117321313895747062088474802365371031
6405990993505000813375432454635967504844235284874701443545419576258473564216198134073468541117668831
0649829795510109541836235030309453097335834462839476304775645015008507578949548931393944899216125525
5406801556035998390548985723546745642390585850216719031395262944554391316631345308939062046784387785
0580717186381054967973100167870850694207092232908070383263453452038027860990556900134137182368370991
8455343729141446513474940784884423772175154334260306698831768331001133108690421939031080143784334151
1919203579582007595605302346267757943936307463056901080114942714100939136913810725813781357894005599
5838758909395688148560263224393726562472776037890814458837855019702843779362407825052704875816470324
4562997651121241536374515005635070127815926714241342103301566165356024733807843028655257222753049998
6806445096986548801682874343786126453815834280753061845485903798217994599681154419742536344399602902
7752723082081063518899152692889108455571126603965034397896278250016110153235160519655904211844949907
9138777817698458758104466283998806006162298486169353373865787735983361613384133853684211978938900185
6231676275475703546994148929041301863861194391962838870543677743224276809132365449485366768000001065
1667766727930354851542040238174608923283917032754257508676551178593950027933895920576682789677644531
0184335607361222765949278393706478426456763388188075656121689605041611390390639601620221536849410926
0167145354315814801054588605645501332037586454858403240298717093480910556211671546848477803944756979
3361833216142802149763399189835484875625298752423873077559555955465196394401821840998412489826236737
0806314077757725705630729400492940302420498416565479736705485580445865720227637840466823379852827105
3958792298185264800706837650418365620945554346135134152570065974881916341359556719649654032187271602
3891375273845892384422535472653098171578447834215822327020690287232330053862163479885094695472004795
2090830733233560348465318730293026659645013718375428897557971449924654038681799213893469244741985097
1562518192155233709607483329234921034514626437449805596103330799414534778457469999212859999939961228
8916145855058397274209809097817293239301067663868240401113040247007350857828724627134946368531815469
8830695976249361510102436555352230690612949388599015734661023712235478911292547696176005047974928060
7820385653909910477594141321543284406250301802757169650820964273484146957263978842560084531214065935
6342423460634237474666080431701260052055928493695941434081468529815053947178900451835755154125223590
4951510198642698878471719396649769070825217423365662725928440620430214113719922785269984698847702323
3640693470437206688651275688266149730788657015685016918647488541679154596507234287730699853713904300
5840667472370297149785084145853085781339156270760356390763947311455495832266945702494139831634332378
6035955402864405902496466930707769055481028850208085800878115773817191741776017330738554758006056014
0327480771811555330909887025505207680463034608658165394876951960044084820659673794731680864156456505
8396645624105195510522357239739512881816405978591427914816542632892004281609136937773722299983327082
9717289822936070288069087768660593252746378405397691848082041021944719713869256084162451123980620113
2479193150856444775379853799732234456122785843296846647513336573692387201464723679427870042503255589
9443158477539700943988394914432353668539209946879645066533985738887866147629443414010498889931600512
5790857466460772283415403114415294188047825438761770790430001566986776795760909966936075594965152736
1796749267844763708474978333655579007384191473198862713525954625181604342253729962863267496824058060
7588815935073578151958899005395120853510357261373640343675347141048360175464883004078464167452167371
6607291248747540316179699411397387765899868554170318847788675929026070043212666179192235209382278788
7048293294140411146540923988344435159133201077394411184074107684981066347241048239358274019449356651
1147318485749233181672072137279355679528443925481560913728128406333039373562420016045664557414588166
1036851321566478001476752310393578606896111259960281839309548709059073861351914591819510297327875571
3703701011049747339493877885989417433031785348707603221982970579751119144051099423588303454635349234
7836272927461561857103721724710095214236964830864102592887457999322374955191221951903424452307535133
2072663917670201183004648190002413083508846584152148991276106513741539435657211390328574918769094413
6076371675054896173016809613803811914361143992106380050832140987604599309324851025168294467260666136